IELTS Master Guide

2024-2025

Beginner to Advanced Writing Skills. Tasks 1 + 2 Academic & General Training

Bands 5-9 for IELTS Academic and General. Includes Essays, Graphs, Tables, Charts, Processes, Maps, Emails, and Letters.

By

Marc Roche

IELTS Writing Consultants

Contents

FREE IELTS Writing Course

Claim your FREE Mini-Course at the end of this book!

Chapter 1. Introduction to IELTS Academic & IELTS General Writing Task 1

"The limits of my language mean the limits of my world." - Ludwig Wittgenstein.

Welcome to your guide on mastering Task 1 of the IELTS Academic and General Writing tests. This section of the book will help you understand the fundamental differences and requirements of each test format.

In Task 1 of the Academic test, you will be asked to analyze and describe information presented in a graph, chart, table, or diagram.

On the other hand, for the General test, you'll need to respond to a situation by writing a letter, which may be personal, semi-formal, or formal.

This introduction will equip you with the skills and strategies needed to effectively organize your thoughts, use appropriate language, and achieve a high score.

Let's begin your journey to becoming proficient.

IELTS Academic Writing Task 1 Overview

In the IELTS writing exam, Tasks 1 and 2 present questions on diverse topics. Each task demands a specific strategy guided by distinct methods and principles. This section is designed to guide you through these strategies, particularly focusing on how to excel in Task 1 of both the IELTS Academic and General Writing tests.

In this section of the book, we guide you step-by-step through the process of writing for Part 1 of the IELTS Academic Writing test.

We've included exercises, tricks, explanations, and examples for:

- Graph descriptions
- Pie chart descriptions
- Map descriptions
- Bar chart descriptions
- Table descriptions
- Process descriptions

IELTS Academic Writing (Source: IELTS.org)

Task	Words	Time	Task description
1	150	20 mins	Describe visual information such as bar tables, charts, graphs, maps, or diagrams.

IELTS General Writing Task 1 Overview

This section shows you what you need in order to write outstanding:

- Emails
- Letters

We will show you how to structure and organize your responses to all types of IELTS General Writing Task 1 questions. Candidates quickly develop fluency and confidence in producing proficient writing under exam conditions.

IELTS General Writing

Task	Words	Time	Task description
1	150	20 mins	Write an email or letter. The style required can be formal, semi-formal, or informal.

How Many Words Should I Write in Task 1 of the IELTS Writing Exam?

- In task 1, you should write **at least** 150 words (no more than 180 words).

- You should spend 20 minutes on it

- This applies to both IELTS Academic and IELTS General.

Two Common Problems in the Exam...

Problem 1- Not Enough Words:

- Less than 150 words might lower your score, as you might not explain your ideas very well.

Problem 2- Too Many Words:

- More than 180 words might be too much.

- You might be using too many words to explain the information. Using **fewer words to express more meaning** is the objective. Not vice-versa.

- You might be trying to express too much without choosing the most important information.

If you write too much:

- You might run out of time during the exam.

- The longer your response is, the more probability you have of making grammar and vocabulary mistakes.

- If you write too many words in Task 1, you will have less time to complete Task 2.

- IELTS ACADEMIC WRITING PART 1-

The IELTS Academic Writing test requires you to write a formal report of 150 words based on visual information.

We have around 20 minutes to complete this task, and it's worth one-third of your overall IELTS Writing test score.

To write a report, you must do three things:

1. Select the main features.

2. Write about the main features.

3. Compare the main features.

The Question

Every question has two sentences and a graphic.

The first sentence gives us a brief description of the graph. Read this part carefully before analyzing the data in the graph, as it will save you time by giving you a good idea about the type of data presented.

The second sentence tells you what you need to do. It tells you how to answer and what information you need to write about.

Before you start writing, read the question and decide what the most important information is.

Example Question:

The chart below shows the number of visitors to three new music museums in the city of Rockville between 2019 and 2022. Summarize the information by selecting and reporting the main features and make comparisons where relevant.

Analysis:

First Sentence Analysis:

The chart below shows the number of visitors to three new music museums in the city of Rockville between 2019 and 2022.

This sentence provides a brief description of the data presented in the graphic. It tells you:

The subject matter: the number of visitors.

The variables being compared are visitors to three different music museums.

The time frame is from 2019 to 2022.

The location: Rockville.

By reading this sentence, you understand that the graphic will display data over a four-year period and will differentiate among three museums. This helps you orient your thinking towards trends over time and comparisons among the museums.

Second Sentence Analysis:

Summarize the information by selecting and reporting the main features and make comparisons where relevant.

This sentence instructs you on how to approach your response:

Task: Summarize the information.

What to focus on: Select and report the main features.

Additional task: Make comparisons where relevant.

This directive tells you not just to list data but to analyze it by highlighting key points like peaks, troughs, similarities, and differences. You should look for overall trends, significant changes over the period, or any anomalies in the data.

The graphic can be:

- a line graph

- a bar chart

- a pie chart

- a table

- a process

- or a map

- In some cases, we might be asked to describe two graphics simultaneously.

We will look at all of these possibilities in this book to prepare you for everything.

Chapter 2. How to Describe Line Graphs in IELTS Academic Writing

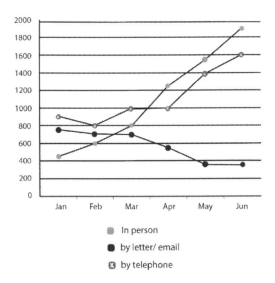

The most common type of Task 1 question in the IELTS Academic exam is the line graph. A line graph consists of data presented along an x and a y-axis and compares how certain numerical variables change over time.

There are several crucial steps to producing a high-scoring IELTS Graph Description. In this section, we will look at how to follow these steps using the following sample question:

WRITING TASK 1

You should spend about **20 minutes** on this task.

The graph below shows the number of enquiries received by a University Admissions Office over a six-month period in 2021.

Summarize the information by selecting and reporting the main features and make comparisons where relevant.

You should write at least 150 words.

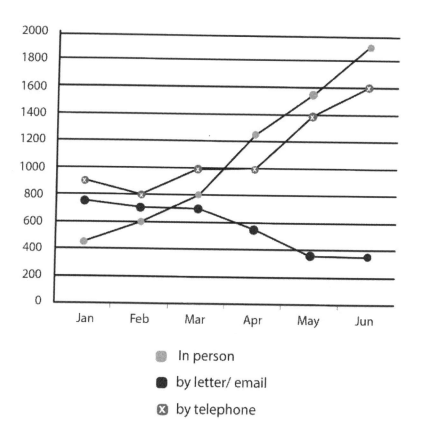

The first step is to analyze the question carefully.

Read the question to understand the type of graph given and what you need to do.

Read the first sentence of the instructions carefully before analyzing the data in the graph, as it will tell you about the type of data presented.

The second sentence tells you what you need to do. It gives you clear instructions on how to answer and what information you need to write about.

The next step is to take a detailed look at the line graph.

Does the data we have represent something from the past or future?

The time period will give you a good idea about the verb tense you need to use in your graph.

Next, you will have to identify what the two axes represent and the units of measurement. Each axis gives a different type of information. These could be many different things, for example, amount, time, age, or percentage.

Examine how the data changes and keep an eye out for notable similarities between data sets. Once you do this, you need to search for the most obvious trends and identify:

- sudden changes

- and areas of stability (where the graph doesn't change).

These pieces of information are the main features that we need to summarize in our report, but how can we describe these features and trends in a concise yet comprehensive manner?

Plan Your Writing

Once our question analysis is complete, we can present the most useful pieces of information in our description.

The typical structure of a graph description is as follows:

Paragraph 1 – Introduce the graph

Paragraph 2 – Give an overview

Paragraph 3 – Present 1st Main Feature

Paragraph 4 – Present 2nd Main Feature

How to Write a Great Introduction

The introduction paragraph of a formal IELTS report is probably one of the easiest parts as long as you practice because it involves simply rephrasing the first line of the question statement.

Take a look at the following example:

Question: The graph below shows the number of enquiries received by the University Admissions Office over a six-month period in 2021.

Paraphrased Sample Introduction: *This line chart represents the number of enquiries made to the University Admissions Office from January to June 2021.*

How To Write A Great Overview

The overview paragraph for any graph description should briefly outline the main trends and features of the graph without going into too many specific details. Use these ideas to form two or three sentences. State the information by simply using synonyms wherever possible.

Sample Overview: *It is clear from the graph that the enquiries made in person and by telephone increased during this time, while the number of enquiries made by email decreased.*

How To Write A Great Main Body Paragraph

In the Main Body Paragraphs, you will give details about the main events mentioned in your Overview. When constructing the main body paragraph(s) of your response, your goal is to communicate the data from the graph in a clear and logical manner. Here are step-by-step instructions to do so:

Detailing Data Points:

Use Exact Figures: Whenever possible, state specific data points (e.g., percentages, numbers). For example, *"In 2015, the number of users increased by 20%, reaching 120,000."*

Estimate When Necessary: If the graph does not provide exact values or if the values are difficult to discern, use approximations. Phrases like "around," "about," "just over," "just under," and "approximately" can be useful. For instance, *"By the end of the decade, the figures had risen to approximately 300,000."*

Highlight Significant Changes: Identify and emphasize major increases, decreases, or periods of stability. Use appropriate verbs and adverbs to describe these trends, such as "gradually increased," "sharply declined," or "remained steady."

Compare and Contrast:

Direct Comparisons: When the graph displays multiple lines, discuss their interactions. For example, *"While the number of users for Product A steadily increased over the period, Product B saw a sharp decline in the first half of the same period."*

Use Comparative Language: Employ comparative adjectives and adverbs like "higher," "lower," "more rapidly," "less significantly," etc., to draw distinctions between different data points or trends.

Time Transitions: Use temporal phrases to guide the reader through the timeline of the data. Phrases like "by the mid-2000s," "towards the end of the period," or "from 2010 to 2020" help set the time frame for your analysis.

Incorporate Data Trends:

Overall Trends: Alongside specific yearly or monthly data, discuss overarching trends throughout the period. For example, *"Over the ten-year period, there was a general upward trend in user numbers."*

Exceptions and Anomalies: Point out any surprising changes or deviations from general trends. This could be a year where the expected growth did not occur or an unexpected peak.

Concluding Sentences: Each paragraph should end with a concise summary or a link to the next paragraph, maintaining a smooth and logical flow. For instance, *"Despite the overall growth, 2018 marked a notable exception, which will be explored further below."*

Exercise: Estimating Quantities

Objective: Practice using approximate quantifiers to describe data accurately in English.

Instructions:

Read the sentences and reference numbers provided.

Fill in the blanks with one of the following words or phrases: "around," "about," "just over," "just under," "approximately." Choose the word or phrase that best fits the context based on the number given.

Explain your choices or write a brief explanation for each choice.

The first sentence has been done for you as an example.

Sentences to Complete:

1. **Example**: The population of our city is *just under* 300,000 people. (Reference: 299,500)

2. The concert lasted _____ three hours last night. (Reference: 3 hours and 10 minutes)

3. The new highway will be _____ 50 miles long. (Reference: 49.8 miles)

4. She earns _____ $40,000 per year at her current job. (Reference: $40,250)

5. The marathon runner completed the race in _____ four hours. (Reference: 4 hours and 5 minutes)

6. Attendance at the annual festival was _____ 10,000 visitors this year. (Reference: 10,050)

7. The cost of the project has risen to _____ $1.2 million due to unexpected expenses. (Reference: $1,199,000)

8. He reads _____ one book per week on average. (Reference: 1 book per 1.2 weeks)

9. The temperature yesterday peaked at _____ 35 degrees Celsius. (Reference: 34.6 degrees Celsius)

10. The small coffee shop sells _____ 75 cups of coffee each day. (Reference: 73 cups)

Extension Task:

Using the same quantifiers, create your own sentences that describe personal experiences or hypothetical scenarios and provide reference numbers for others to guess the correct quantifier.

Answer Key

1. The population of our city is just under 300,000 people.

    Explanation: 299,500 is slightly less than 300,000, hence "just under."

2. The concert lasted just over three hours last night.

    Explanation: 3 hours and 10 minutes is slightly more than three hours, so "just over" is appropriate.

3. The new highway will be just under 50 miles long.

    Explanation: 49.8 miles is very close to, but still less than 50 miles.

4. She earns just over $40,000 per year at her current job.

    Explanation: $40,250 is slightly more than $40,000.

5. The marathon runner completed the race in just over four hours.

    Explanation: Completing the race in 4 hours and 5 minutes is slightly over four hours.

6. Attendance at the annual festival was just over 10,000 visitors this year.

    Explanation: 10,050 is slightly above 10,000, fitting "just over."

7. The cost of the project has risen to just under $1.2 million due to unexpected expenses.

    Explanation: $1,199,000 is very close to but not reaching $1.2 million, hence "just under."

8. He reads approximately one book per week on average.

Explanation: Reading one book every 1.2 weeks suggests some weeks he might not finish a book, thus "approximately" indicates this slight variability.

9. The temperature yesterday peaked at just under 35 degrees Celsius.

   Explanation: 34.6 degrees is very close to 35 degrees but not quite there, so "just under" is suitable.

10. The small coffee shop sells just under 75 cups of coffee each day.

    Explanation: Selling 73 cups is close to but less than 75, making "just under" the right choice.

Step-by-Step Practice

WRITING TASK 1

You should spend about 20 minutes on this task.

The graph below shows the number of enquiries received by a University Admissions Office over a six-month period in 2021.

Summarize the information by selecting and reporting the main features and make comparisons where relevant.

You should write at least 150 words.

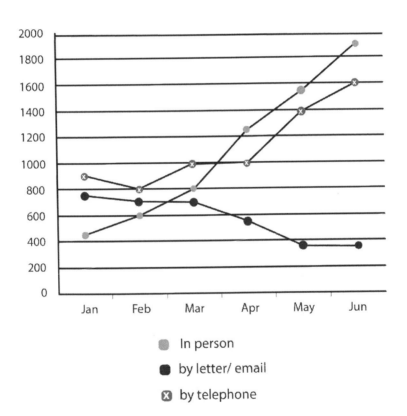

Exercise 1: Summarizing the Main Points

Objective: Practice writing an introductory sentence that summarizes the main points of the graph.

Task: Rewrite the introductory sentence of the following sample, ensuring it captures the essence of the graph's data without specific figures.

Sample Sentence: *"The line graph represents the number of enquiries made to a University Admissions Office from January to June 2021."*

Your Task: Write two alternative introductory sentences.

Write here:

1. The line graph represents the number of enquiries recieved by a University admissions from Jan- Jun of 2021.

2. The line graph represents the number of enquiries made to a University admissions office during a 6 month period in 2021.

Exercise 2: Describing Trends Accurately

Objective: Learn to describe trends using precise vocabulary.

Task: The sample describes various changes in the number of enquiries. Rewrite these descriptions using different verbs and adjectives.

Original Descriptions:

"In-person enquiries rose sharply from around 400 to 1900."

"Enquiries made by telephone showed a more gradual increase."

"Enquiries by email showed an opposite trend, steadily declining from around 800 to around 400 enquiries."

Your Task: Provide alternative descriptions for each trend using new verbs and adjectives.

Write here:

1. In person enquiries sharply increased from 400 to 1900.

2. Enquiries made by telephone had a more gradual increase.

3.

Exercise 3: Using Comparative Language

Objective: Practice using comparative language to highlight differences in trends.

Task: Compare the trends for the three types of enquiries using comparative language.

Sample: *"In contrast, enquiries by email showed an opposite trend, steadily declining from around 800 to around 400 enquiries."*

Your Task: Write a sentence that compares the trend in telephone enquiries to both in-person and email enquiries.

Write here:

Exercise 4: Data Detail and Precision

Objective: Improve precision in describing data from the graph.

Task: The sample provides specific numbers at different points in the graph. Practice providing these details with accuracy.

Sample Details:

"Initially, telephone enquiries declined slightly from 900 to 800 enquiries, before increasing to 1000 in the third month."

Your Task: Choose a month and describe the change in enquiries for that month using precise numbers and descriptive words.

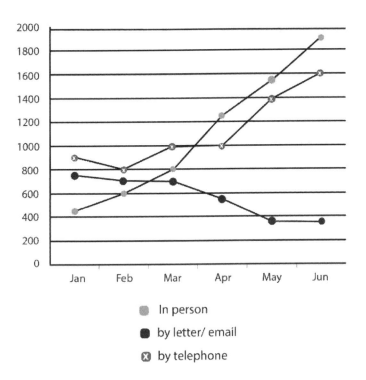

- In person
- by letter/ email
- by telephone

Sample Task 1 Line Graph Response

The line graph represents the number of enquiries made to a University Admissions Office from January to June 2021.

It is clear from the graph that the enquiries made in person and by telephone increased during this time, while the number of enquiries made by email decreased.

According to what is shown in the graph, in-person enquiries rose sharply from around 400 to 1900, while enquiries made by telephone showed a more gradual increase. Initially, telephone enquiries declined slightly from 900 to 800 enquiries, before increasing to 1000 in the third month. The ratio remained at this level for the month of April and then increased substantially in May and June to reach 1600 enquiries by the end of the period.

In contrast, enquiries by email showed an opposite trend, steadily declining from around 800 to around 400 enquiries over the 6-month period.

IELTS Graph Language Exercise

Let's focus on expanding your range of vocabulary and grammar structures to summarize changes shown within a graph.

Match the words with their corresponding images below. More than one option is possible.

A. Rose steadily/increased steadily/grew steadily

B. Rose dramatically/increased dramatically/grew dramatically

C. Plummeted to/Plunged to …

D. Hit a peak of, peaked at, or reached a high of …

E. Fluctuated, varied, or oscillated/Became erratic. Was erratic/inconsistent

F. Dropped/Shrank/Fell drastically/ sharply dramatically

G. Remained flat/unchanged/stable/constant at

H. Dropped and then stabilized/evened out at

I. Hit a low of …/ bottomed out at

J. Dropped and then quickly recovered

K. Dipped/ Declined slightly before quickly recovering

L. Rocketed / Soared

M. Fell slowly/ gradually / steadily

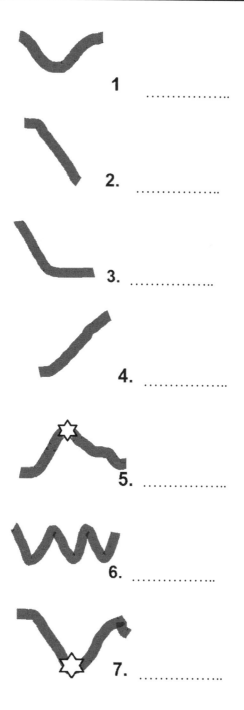

1 ....

2. ....

3. ....

4. ....

5. ....

6. ....

7. ....

8. ....

9. ....

10. ....

Answers

1. *Fell and then quickly recovered / Dipped/ fell slightly*

2. *Fell/ dropped/ shrank drastically/ dramatically / sharply/ Plummeted to/ Plunged to*

3. *Dropped and then leveled off/ evened out at*

4. *Rose/ increased dramatically/ Soared/ Rocketed*

5. *Hit a peak / Peaked at/ reached a high of*

6. *Fluctuated/ was erratic*

7. *Hit a low of …*

8. *Rose/ increased steadily/ Rose/ increased gradually*

9. *Remained flat/ constant/ unchanged/ stable at*

10. *Fell gradually / steadily*

Please note that these are only some of the options from the table.

IELTS Graph Language Notes

Word	Explanation
Dipped	Fell slightly but recovered quickly
Bottomed out / Hit a low of	The lowest point on the graph
Plummeted to... / Plunged to	Suffered a quick and drastic or shocking decrease. Fell extremely quickly. A drastic fall or reduction
Fluctuated / was erratic	Increases and decreases randomly, irregularly, or unpredictably
Rose/increased dramatically/ Soared/ Rocketed	Increased very quickly and drastically
Peaked at / reached a high of	The highest point on the graph

Remained constant/unchanged/stable at ..../ Leveled off/evened out at ...	a part of the graph where there is no change

Writing Practice

The graph below gives information about changes in the birth and death rates in New Zealand between 1901 and 2101.

Summarise the information by selecting and reporting the main features, and make comparisons where relevant.

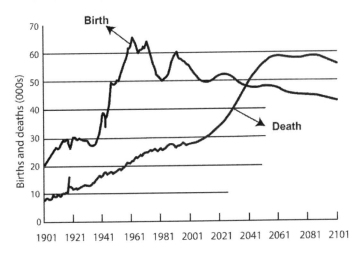

Source:

http://archive.stats.govt.nz/browse_for_stats/population/estimates_and_projections/changing-face-of-nzs-population.aspx

Exercise instructions: Write 150-180 words below. You can compare your answer to the Sample Response on the next page:

Sample Response

The line graph shows the historical and predicted trends for the rate of birth and mortality in New Zealand for the period from 1901 through to 2101.

At the start of the review period, the birth rate surpasses the mortality rate. The forecasted data shows that the mortality rate is likely to exceed the birth rate by 2041, at which point, the large gap between the two will level off.

At the beginning of the period, the birth rate started at 20,000, peaking at around 66,000 in 1961 before fluctuating between 50,000 and 65,000 until 2021. It is anticipated to decline to around 45,000 births by 2101 slowly.

In contrast, the mortality rate started at just below 10,000 in 1901 and steadily rose throughout, reaching around 30,000 in 2021. This increase is expected to accelerate between 2021 and 2041, when the number of deaths will surpass the number of births. By 2051, the death rate will stabilize at around 60,000 and decline marginally until the end of the period.

Useful Language for Graph Descriptions

- *...significantly declined...*

- *...remained the same...*

- *...reached a plateau...*

- *...rose dramatically...*

- *...fell slightly...*

- *...fluctuated...*

- *...increased steadily...*

- *...fell gradually...*

- *...decreased steadily...*

- *...remained stable...*

- *...recovered...*

- *...fluctuated dramatically...*

- *...rocketed...*

- *...plunged...*

- *...a dramatic fall...*

- *...a period of stability...*

- *...a slight dip...*

- *...it doubled...*

- *...it halved...*

- *...increased sevenfold (7 times)*

- *...increased fourfold (4 times)*

- *...proved to be the most popular...*

- *...began the year higher; however, by the end of the year ...*

- *...followed the same sales trend...*

- *...were consistently the lowest...*

- *...A similar pattern is also noted on...*

- *...With regards to...*

- *...is similar/ dissimilar...*

Structures for Summarizing Change

If you want to achieve great results, you need to learn more than just one structure for summarizing change. You must add an element of variety to your writing when you are describing shifts in data. This will not only keep your reader engaged, but it will also help to demonstrate a higher level of knowledge. It will give a better impression of your abilities as a communicator.

Be mindful of using the correct word forms when you are building your sentences. Lapses in concentration can cause some writers to confuse adjectives such as progressive with their adverb form progressively.

The following resource tables contain the language to describe pretty much any graph which involves changes over time.

There + be + adjective + noun + in + noun
There was a slow rise in the number of kilograms consumed.
There was a dramatic rise in the amount of oil produced.
There was a sharp jump in ice cream sales.
There has been a considerable increase in the number of languages

spoken within the region since 1980.
There was a slight increase in the number of cars sold.
There was a sharp fall in the number of loans offered.
There was a dramatic fluctuation in the amount of rice consumed.

Noun + verb + adverb
Fast food consumption rose steadily.
The number of people claiming unemployment benefits rose considerably between 2008 and 2011.
The value of gold decreased slightly during the period.
The figures declined slightly, dropping to 44,000 in 2012.

Time + saw/experienced/witnessed + adjective + noun + in + noun
*there is no preposition before time words in this structure (Never: *In* + time + *saw...*)
2003 saw a gradual increase in oil consumption.
2009 saw a sudden plunge in ice-cream sales to 20,000.
The end of the period saw a gradual decline in the figures, dropping to 44,000 in 2012.
The decade ended pretty much the same as it began, with an average consumption of just over 20lb per household.

Verb-Adverb Combinations

Verb	Adverb
fell	*minimally / gradually / rapidly / dramatically / slowly / markedly / sharply*
declined	*minimally / gradually / rapidly / dramatically / slowly / markedly / sharply*
shrank	*minimally / gradually / rapidly / dramatically / slowly / markedly / sharply*
dropped	*minimally / gradually / rapidly / dramatically / slowly / markedly / sharply*
rose	*rapidly / gradually / rapidly / dramatically / slowly*
increased	*rapidly / dramatically / slowly / gradually*
grew	*slightly / steadily / suddenly / gradually*
fluctuated	*wildly / slightly / suddenly*
jumped	*erratically / slightly / dramatically*
plunged	*suddenly / unexpectedly*
soared	*suddenly / unexpectedly*

Cheat Sheet (IELTS Academic Writing Part 1)

1. Focus on Clear Data Description

Use precise language: It's crucial to describe data accurately. Phrases like "a significant increase," "remained stable," or "a slight decline" are useful. Avoid ambiguous terms that don't specifically describe the data trends.

Select relevant details: Identify the most important trends, comparisons, and changes. Don't try to describe every single detail in the graph or chart.

2. Organize Your Response Effectively

Introduction: Briefly paraphrase the question to introduce your essay. For example, if the prompt says, "The chart below shows the number of visitors...," you could start with, "The provided chart illustrates the visitor numbers..."

Overview: Include a general summary of the main information or prominent trends without specific data. This could be the differences over time, highs and lows, or general trends.

Body paragraphs: Divide the data into logical sections. For example, discuss each line on a graph in a separate paragraph or divide the time periods into different sections. Use clear topic sentences to introduce the focus of each paragraph.

3. Maintain Analytical Tone

Use comparative language: When discussing two or more data points, use comparative forms, such as "greater than," "less than," or "equivalent to," to highlight differences or similarities.

Be objective: Keep your tone formal and academic. Avoid inserting personal opinions or assumptions about the data.

4. Practice Time Management

Timed practice: The Writing Part 1 should ideally take about 20 minutes. Practice with a timer to ensure you can comfortably plan, write, and review your response within this timeframe.

Review and revise: Reserve the last 3-5 minutes to check for and correct any grammatical errors or typos. This review phase can significantly enhance the quality of your final submission.

5. Enhance Vocabulary for Describing Trends

Learn key verbs and nouns: Verbs like "increase," "decline," "peak," "fluctuate," and nouns like "peak," "trough," and "plateau" are valuable.

Adverbs and adjectives: Use adverbs and adjectives to describe the extent of change, such as "dramatically," "moderately," and "slightly."

6. Use Graph-Specific Vocabulary

Understand terms specific to graphs and charts: Words like "axis," "interval," "frequency," and "scale" should be well understood and correctly used.

Chapter 3. Bar Charts

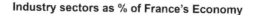

Industry sectors as % of France's Economy

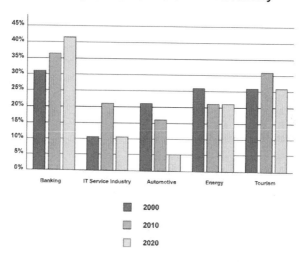

Bar graphs are another of the most common types of questions asked during the IELTS Academic Writing test. For this type of question, you will be presented with an image of a bar chart and asked to describe the main features of this graph within a formal report of at least 150 words.

As with any other IELTS Writing Task One, you have around 20 minutes for this task and it's worth **one third** of your IELTS Writing test score.

The bars are colored or symbol-marked rectangular blocks representing certain variables that can be compared, like in the following example:

Industry sectors as % of France's Economy

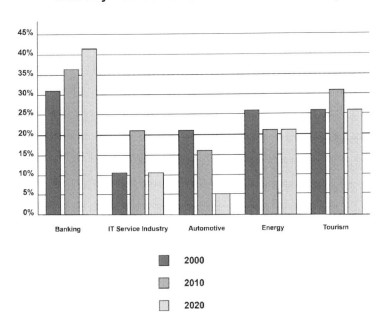

- They can be placed in a horizontal or vertical position.

- These types of graphs usually represent the rate of change of certain variables concerning time.

- The information presented in bar charts is not necessarily dependent on any other variables, and the data on the x-axis can be grouped by category. For example: Spending Type, Disease Type, etc.

- So, it's important to use effective vocabulary to express these trends in words. You might have to describe periods of sudden changes (both upwards and downwards) or periods of stability.

This section reveals the steps you need to follow to write a high-scoring IELTS bar chart report. We will use the following sample question.

You should spend about 20 minutes on this task.

The chart shows components of GDP in Australia from 2012 to 2020. Summarize the information by selecting and reporting the main features and make comparisons where relevant.

Write at least 150 words.

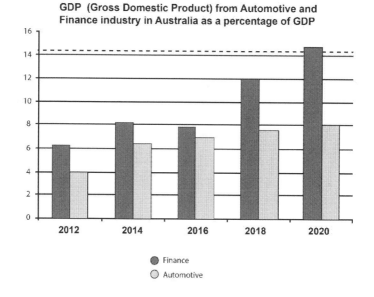

Analyze The Question

As always, it is important to read the question carefully before analyzing the data.

- Doing this ensures that you answer the question fully, which is an integral part of your final score.

- Every bar graph question consists of a brief description of the graphic, and the instructions that tell you what you have to do, along with the bar chart. This gives us a great idea about the kind of data we will see.

- Make sure you understand what each bar and axis represent.

- The question statement also gives us exactly how to answer and what information we need to give the examiner within our description.

- You need to note down the main features of the graph, and you should also take note of any comparisons that can be made between the bars.

Plan Your Report

Next, we need to organize the information we've gathered during our question analysis and decide on how to lay out the most useful parts with our report.

The typical structure for a formal bar graph report is:

Paragraph 1 – Paraphrase the question

Paragraph 2 – Give an Overview

Paragraph 3 – Describe Main Feature 1

Write a Great Introduction

Paraphrase the first sentence of the question. Try to reorder the words and use synonyms wherever appropriate. For example:

Question words: *The chart shows components of GDP in Australia from 2012 to 2020.*

Our introduction is as follows:

The bar chart illustrates the percentage of Gross Domestic Product from the Automotive and Finance industries in Australia between 2012 and 2020.

Tips for Paraphrasing:

Use synonyms: Replace words with their synonyms where possible without changing the meaning. For example, "shows" can be changed to "depicts," "illustrates," or "presents."

Change the structure: Alter the sentence structure. For instance, if the original sentence starts with "The chart shows," you might start with "Presented in the bar chart is..."

Adjust the grammar: Sometimes, changing the voice from active to passive or vice versa can help in paraphrasing effectively.

Focus on clarity: Ensure that the paraphrased sentence is not only different in words but also clear and correct in its presentation of the original information.

Exercise: Writing the Perfect Introduction for a Bar Chart Description

Objective: Develop the ability to paraphrase the prompt effectively to create a clear, engaging introduction for a bar chart description.

Instructions:

Read the example question and introduction provided.

Complete the exercises below by rewriting the given questions into introductory sentences for an IELTS bar chart description.

Example Question and Introduction:

Question: The chart shows components of GDP in Australia from 2012 to 2020.

Introduction: *The bar chart depicts the percentage of Gross Domestic Product from the Automotive and Finance industries in Australia between 2012 and 2020.*

Your Task:

Question 1: The bar chart illustrates the distribution of market shares among leading smartphone manufacturers over the last decade.

Your Introduction: (Write your paraphrased introduction here)

Question 2: The graph displays changes in the number of public libraries in Europe from 2000 to 2015.

Your Introduction: (Write your paraphrased introduction here)

Question 3: The diagram outlines the average cost of residential properties in major cities around the world as of last year.

Your Introduction: (Write your paraphrased introduction here)

Question 4: The chart presents the annual revenue generated by three major video streaming services from 2015 to 2022.

Your Introduction: (Write your paraphrased introduction here)

Question 5: The graph indicates the percentage of renewable energy used in electricity production in different continents from 1990 to 2020.

Your Introduction: (Write your paraphrased introduction here)

Answers

Question 1: The bar chart illustrates the distribution of market shares among leading smartphone manufacturers over the last decade.

Your Introduction: The diagram depicts the market share percentages held by top smartphone brands throughout the past ten years.

Question 2: The graph displays changes in the number of public libraries in Europe from 2000 to 2015.

Your Introduction: The bar chart shows variations in the total count of public libraries across Europe between the years 2000 and 2015.

Question 3: The diagram outlines the average cost of residential properties in major cities around the world as of last year.

Your Introduction: The graph presents a comparison of the average residential property prices in key global cities as recorded last year.

Question 4: The chart presents the annual revenue generated by three major video streaming services from 2015 to 2022.

Your Introduction: The bar chart illustrates the yearly revenue figures for three leading video streaming platforms from 2015 through 2022.

Question 5: The graph indicates the percentage of renewable energy used in electricity production in different continents from 1990 to 2020.

Your Introduction: Presented in the bar chart is the proportion of renewable energy sources employed in electricity generation across various continents over the period from 1990 to 2020.

Write a Great Overview

An overview is a statement of the general trends found within a graph. You do not need to mention specific numbers or details in an overview, and it is usually just one or two sentences long. It would be sufficient to mention the overall trends, such as a *downward* or *upward* trend or an *overall period of stability*.

For example:

Overall, it can be seen that although both categories increased as a percentage of GDP, Finance had much more significant growth in ratio during the given time period.

Here is a short exercise to help you practice writing a great overview for the IELTS Writing Task 1:

Exercise: Writing a Great Overview for Bar Charts

Objective: Develop the ability to identify and succinctly summarize the general trends observed in a bar chart without citing specific data.

Instructions:

Read the descriptions of the bar charts provided below. Each description highlights different data trends.

Write a one to two-sentence overview for each scenario, focusing on the main trends rather than specific numbers.

Example Scenarios:

Scenario 1:

The bar chart compares the number of cars sold by three different brands (Brand A, Brand B, Brand C) over four quarters in a year. Brand A and Brand B show gradual increases each quarter, while Brand C's sales peak in the second quarter and then significantly decline.

Scenario 2:

The chart shows the amount of waste recycled in four cities (City X, City Y, City Z, City W) over five years. While Cities X and Y show a steady increase in recycling, City Z shows little change, and City W initially increases but then decreases in the last year.

Scenario 3:

This bar chart illustrates the total hours spent on social media per week in different age groups (Teenagers, Young Adults, Adults, Seniors). There is a clear downward trend as age increases, with Teenagers spending the most time and Seniors the least.

Scenario 4:

The chart outlines annual visitor numbers to three museums (Museum L, Museum M, Museum N) over a decade. All museums show growth in visitor numbers, but Museum N shows the fastest growth rate, doubling its visitors in the period.

Answer Key: Writing Overviews for Bar Charts

Scenario 1 Overview:

"Overall, the sales trends for Brand A and Brand B consistently increased throughout the year, whereas Brand C experienced a peak in sales in the second quarter followed by a significant decline."

Scenario 2 Overview:

"Overall, Cities X and Y demonstrated a progressive increase in recycled waste over the five-year period, contrasting with the stable levels in City Z and the fluctuating figures in City W."

Scenario 3 Overview:

"The chart reveals a distinct trend where total hours spent on social media decrease with age, with Teenagers showing the highest engagement and Seniors the least."

Scenario 4 Overview:

"Overall, all three museums saw an increase in visitors over the decade, with Museum N exhibiting the most rapid growth."

Write The Main Body

For the 3rd and 4th paragraphs, you will extend the main ideas mentioned in your overview. Here, you should add more details in the form of exact figures and information to support the main ideas and trends mentioned in your overview. Remember to compare and contrast as well. When giving specific data, you have to include exact numbers/percentages and include as many details as possible. Since the exact numbers might be difficult to read in some cases, you can use words like *around, about,* and *approximately*.

Take a look at the following sample main body paragraphs. Pay attention to how we've used the language in bold:

To begin, *in 2012, the Finance industry started at 6%,* ***whereas*** *the Automotive Industry* ***accounted for*** *4% of the total GDP. During the next four years, the* ***levels*** *for both categories* ***remained relatively stable at around*** *6% and 8%, with the Finance sector* ***remaining slightly higher overall***, *despite a small decrease between 2014 and 2016.*

However, *a considerable change can be seen between the two categories in the next four years of the given period. The income generated from the Finance sector increased dramatically to 12% in 2018 and then nearly 15% in 2020,* ***while*** *the Automotive Industry* ***saw little change***, *increasing to only 8%.* ***By the end of the period***, *the GDP percentage from the Finance sector* ***was nearly double that of the*** *Automotive industry at 15% and 8%* ***respectively***.

Full Sample Response

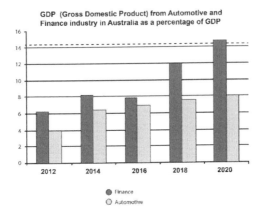

GDP (Gross Domestic Product) from Automotive and Finance industry in Australia as a percentage of GDP

● Finance
○ Automotive

The bar chart depicts the percentage of Gross Domestic Product from the Automotive and Finance industries in Australia between 2012 and 2020.

Overall, it can be seen that although both categories increased as a percentage of GDP, Finance had much more significant growth in ratio during the given time period.

To begin, in 2012, the Finance industry started at 6%, whereas the Automotive Industry accounted for 4% of the total GDP. During the next four years, the levels for both categories remained relatively stable at around 6% and 8%, with the Finance sector remaining slightly higher overall, despite a small decrease between 2014 and 2016.

However, a considerable change can be seen between the two categories in the next four years of the given period. The income generated from the Finance sector increased dramatically to 12% in 2018 and then nearly 15% in 2020, while the Automotive Industry saw little change, increasing to only 8 %. By the end of the period, the GDP percentage from the Finance sector was nearly double that of the Automotive industry at 15% and 8% respectively.

Adding Transitions to Your Sentences

➤ *The U.S. produces over 2.2 billion tons of wheat every year.* **In contrast,** *Russia produces just over half a billion per year.*

➤ *Italy produced large amounts of dairy products.* **In comparison,** *Thailand produced very little.*

➤ *Finland imports some 10 million tons of flour per year* **but** *produces none.*

Note: remember the word *some* can be used to mean *about/around*, so you can use it to add variety to your writing.

While/Whereas/Although/Though

These words are great for adding transitions within sentences without having to add a full stop and write a new sentence. They allow you to compare and contrast while keeping your text fluid and readable.

➤ *Although Italy produces over 6 million tons of olives, Spain produces almost double that amount.*

➤ *Spain produces high levels of solar power,* **whereas/while** *Japan produces almost none.*

➤ *While Germany consumes nearly 80 million tons of rice per year, it produces none.*

Comparing and Contrasting Similar Data

➤ *Austria produced* **the same** *amount of butter as Switzerland.*

➤ **Like** *Thailand, Malaysia produces 30,000 bottles.*

➤ *India consumes over 100 million tons of rice per year.* **Likewise,/ Similarly,** *China consumes 118.8 million.*

➤ **Both** *India and China consume over 100 million tons of rice per year.*

➤ **Both** *the UK and Spain produce medium levels of carbon emissions.*

Exercise

Put the terms in **bold** in the right gap. Then, check your answers on the next page.

remained relatively stable

To begin,

levels

will see little change

Whereas

while

However

Around

remaining slightly higher overall

accounted for

.................., in 2010, the Online Retail industry started at 11%, ... the Highstreet Retail industry .... 7% of total investment.

During the next decade, the .... for both industries .... at ....15% and 8%, with the Online Retail sector ...., despite a small decrease between 2019 and 2020.

........................, a considerable change is expected between the two categories in the next ten years. Investment in the Online Retail sector will increase dramatically to 33% by 2025 and then nearly 45% in 2030, ... the Highstreet Retail sector ...., increasing to only 10%.

Answers

To begin with, in 2010, the online retail industry started at 11%, *whereas* the high street retail industry **accounted for** 7% of total investment.

During the next decade, the **levels** *for both industries* **remained relatively stable** *at* **around** *15% and 8%, with the Online Retail sector* **remaining slightly higher overall**, *despite a small decrease between 2019 and 2020.*

However, *a considerable change is expected between the two categories in the next ten years. Investment in the Online Retail sector will increase dramatically to 33% by 2025 and then nearly 45% in 2030,* **while** *the Highstreet Retail sector* **will see little change**, *increasing to only 10%.*

Writing Practice

The following chart shows five different industries' percentage share of France's economy in 2000, 2010, and 2020.

Summarise the information by selecting and reporting the main features, and make comparisons where relevant.

Industry sectors as % of France's Economy

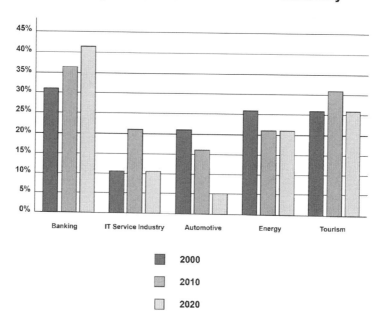

Exercise instructions: Write your response and compare it to *Full Sample Response 2* on the next page.

Write 150-180 words below:

Sample Response

The bar graph depicts the actual shares of the French economy held by five major business sectors in 2000, 2010, and 2020.

Of the five sectors, banking had the most growth, with a 30% market share in 2000, 35% in 2010, and just over 40% in 2020. In contrast, the automotive sector's contribution decreased over the years, from 20% in 2000 to 5% in 2020.

The IT Service Industry, which accounted for about 10% of the economy in 2000, grew in 2010 but declined back to its original level in 2020 at 10%. Similarly, tourism grew by 5% between 2000 and 2010 but then shrank to its original 25% by 2020. The Energy sector, which was booming in 2000 with a share of around 25%, dropped slightly by 5% and remained at the same level in the last decade.

In summary, for the period, banking accounted for the biggest share of France's economy, with steady growth from 2000 to 2020, while the automotive industry accounted for the smallest share of the economy, experiencing a steady decline throughout the period.

Chapter 4. Pie Chart Descriptions in IELTS Academic Writing

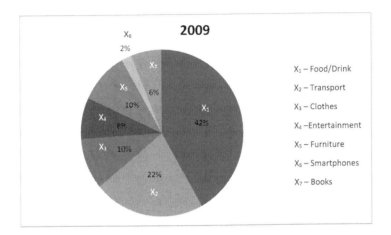

As we've seen in previous chapters, you will be asked to write a formal report of about 150 words during the Academic IELTS writing exam. This report will usually be based on information derived from some form of a graph, including line or bar graphs and pie charts.

This chapter will take an in-depth look at how to write a high-scoring report on a pie chart and offer some valuable tips and insights into exactly what the IELTS examiners look for in a well-written pie chart description.

What Is A Pie Chart?

A pie chart is a circle divided into various sectors, where each sector represents a part of a whole. It depicts several percentages and proportions; there are no x and y axes, but there is usually a color-coded or a symbol-coded key for each sector.

A pie chart displays information in an easy-to-understand way and makes it simple to compare data from multiple categories.

In most IELTS Task 1 questions, you will get pie charts representing different categories or the changes in certain sectors between two or more years.

How to Write a Pie Chart Description

Writing a pie chart description is very similar to the methods used for a bar chart report.

You need to

- Analyze the question

- Plan out your report structure

- Write a good introduction

- Write an overview paragraph

- Write the main body paragraphs

Analyze The Question.

- Before you rush into writing your report, it is important to read the question carefully and inspect the pie charts.

- You need to extract and interpret as much information as you can from the question statement, titles, and labels, as well as the units of measurement.

- Many candidates assume that the figures represent percentages, but this is not always the case.

- You should also take note of major differences and similarities between different sectors since pie charts require a significant amount of comparison instead of just listing the figures for each sector.

We will use the following sample question to illustrate these points. This is the same example we use in the IELTS Writing Band 9 Video Course on our website.

Sample Instructions:

The charts below show the proportions of consumer expenditure by sector.

Summarize the information by selecting and reporting the main features and make comparisons where relevant.

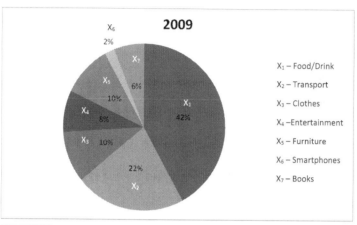

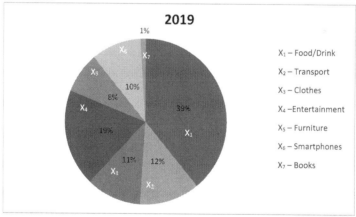

By looking at the pie charts as well as the headings, we can see that:

- These charts show data about consumer spending

- There are seven different categories

- The figures are measured in percentages

- There are two time periods shown, which are both in the past.

Now, we need to look for some main features :

- The category of Food/Drink represented the main expense for people in both years

- In 2009, people spent a lot on transport, but this figure decreased a lot by 2019

- Entertainment more than doubled to become the second-highest expense by 2019.

- People spent the least on books in both periods, but the figure was significantly lower in 2019

Write a Great Introduction

A writing task 1 introduction paragraph is probably one of the easiest paragraphs to write during the IELTS test because it involves simply paraphrasing the first line of the question statement. However, as in all the other types of task 1, copying the question word for word will give the examiner the impression that you do not have a wide enough vocabulary. So, make sure to use appropriate synonyms instead.

Question Statement: The charts below show the proportions of consumer expenditure by sector.

Sample Introduction: *The pie charts depict consumer spending habits for seven categories in 2009 and 2019.*

Tips for Paraphrasing:

Use synonyms for verbs and nouns ("shows" can become "depicts," "illustrates," "outlines"; "proportions" can become "percentages" or "ratios").

You can change the grammatical structure (e.g., "*The pie chart shows*" could be rewritten as "*Displayed in the pie chart are*").

Aim to make the introduction engaging and informative without delving into specific details, which are reserved for the body of the response.

Exercise: Writing an Introduction for a Pie Chart Description

Objective: Develop skills in writing an effective introduction for pie chart descriptions by paraphrasing the question prompts.

Instructions:

Read the example pie chart question prompts provided below.

Write a paraphrased introduction for each prompt, focusing on clarity and effective use of synonyms while maintaining the original meaning.

Example Question Prompts:

Prompt 1:

The pie chart shows the proportions of the population in a small town who prefer different genres of movies.

Prompt 2:

The pie chart illustrates the percentage of market share held by different computer brands in 2020.

Prompt 3:

The pie chart displays the distribution of government spending on public services in 2019.

Prompt 4:

The pie chart outlines how students at a university commute to campus.

Prompt 5:

The pie chart represents the various sources of energy production in Country X.

Answers

Prompt 1:

Paraphrased Introduction: *"The pie chart presents the various movie genre preferences among the residents of a small town."*

Prompt 2:

Paraphrased Introduction: *"The pie chart delineates the market share distribution among various computer brands in the year 2020."*

Prompt 3:

Paraphrased Introduction: *"Presented in the pie chart is the breakdown of how the government allocated funds across different public services in 2019."*

Prompt 4:

Paraphrased Introduction: *"The pie chart depicts the various modes of transportation used by students to commute to university."*

Prompt 5:

Paraphrased Introduction: *"The pie chart illustrates the different sources of energy production utilized in Country X."*

Write a Great Overview Paragraph

In your overview paragraph, you need to mention, in 1 or 2 lines, the main trends and features that you noted down during your question analysis. Remember that you do not need to go into too much detail in this paragraph.

Sample Overview: *It is clear from the charts that people spent the most on food and drink and the least on books in both years and that people spent a significantly higher amount on entertainment in 2019 than they did in 2009.*

Exercise: Writing a Great Overview Paragraph for Pie Chart Descriptions

Objective: Develop the ability to synthesize key information from a pie chart prompt into a concise overview that highlights major trends and notable features.

Instructions:

Read the pie chart prompts and their descriptions below.

Write a one or two-sentence overview for each, focusing on the essential trends or notable features indicated by the prompt.

Example Solution for Scenario 1:

Overview: *"The pie chart indicates that a substantial portion of daily internet usage in an urban setting is devoted to social media and entertainment, while study-related activities occupy a minimal percentage."*

Pie Chart Scenarios and Prompts:

Scenario 1:

Prompt: The pie chart shows the percentage breakdown of daily internet usage by activity (social media, work, study, entertainment, other) in a typical urban population.

Description: The chart reveals a high percentage of usage for social media and entertainment, with minimal use for study.

Scenario 2:

Prompt: The pie chart illustrates the distribution of budget spending by a local government on different sectors: education, healthcare, infrastructure, public safety, and environmental conservation.

Description: Education and public safety take up most of the budget, with environmental conservation receiving the least funding.

Scenario 3:

Prompt: The pie chart displays the proportions of beverages (coffee, tea, soda, water) sold in a cafe during a month.

Description: Coffee sales dominate the chart, while soda holds the smallest share.

Scenario 4:

Prompt: The pie chart outlines the market share of four major smartphone operating systems.

Description: Two operating systems dominate the market equally, while the other two have significantly smaller shares.

Scenario 5:

Prompt: "The pie chart represents the division of time spent by an average teenager on various weekday activities: sleep, school, homework, sports, and leisure."

Description: Most time is spent in school and sleeping, with very little time allocated to sports.

Answers

Scenario 1:

Overview: *"The pie chart clearly shows that social media and entertainment account for the majority of daily internet usage in a typical urban setting, with study activities being notably less frequent."*

Scenario 2:

Overview: *"It is evident from the pie chart that the local government allocates the majority of its budget to education and public safety, while environmental conservation receives the smallest share of funding."*

Scenario 3:

Overview: *"The pie chart demonstrates that coffee is the predominant beverage sold in the cafe, significantly outselling the least popular beverage, soda."*

Scenario 4:

Overview: *"The pie chart reveals a market predominantly divided between two major smartphone operating systems, with the remaining two systems capturing much smaller shares."*

Scenario 5:

Overview: *"According to the pie chart, the majority of a teenager's weekday is consumed by school and sleep, with minimal time dedicated to sports."*

Write The Main Body

In these paragraphs, you need to describe the information mentioned in your overview paragraph in greater detail, using facts, figures, and periods if relevant.

When you get two pie charts like this, you can use a separate paragraph for each one or directly compare, using language like *whereas, while,* etc. For the sake of this explanation, we will use separate paragraphs, as they help organize the report and avoid confusion. A good way of approaching this task is to write your report as if the reader has not seen the pie chart and is using only your report to understand the information in the graph.

It is also important to note that you cannot use phrases like *decrease gradually* or *increase sharply* for pie charts since the values are usually fixed and not measured over long periods. Many students make this error, and it just gives the impression that the candidate used words and phrases without fully understanding their meaning and usage. Remember, you should not use complicated words that you do not understand. This will not help you score higher; it will almost guarantee a lower score on the IELTS exam. Your report must be easy to follow and understand, and you have to use natural-sounding phrases that a native speaker would use and understand.

Sample Main Body Paragraphs:

According to what is shown, the category of Food/Drink was the main expense for people in both years at 42% and 39% respectively. In 2009, transport was the second-highest expense at 22%. Clothes and furniture had the same ratio of 10%, and people spent the smallest amount of their income on books at 6 percent.

In 2019 there were a few changes in consumer spending patterns. People spent the most on food and drink, but at a value of 3% lower than in 2009, while entertainment became the second-highest expense in 2019, with a substantial increase from 8% in 2009 to 19% in 2009. The books category witnessed a significant decrease to just 1% of the total consumer expenditure.

Once you have written your main body paragraphs, make sure to thoroughly recheck your work for spelling, punctuation, and grammatical errors. Careless mistakes can cause a lack of clarity in your report and lower your score.

You can start practicing now that you have a solid strategy to answer pie chart descriptions. Remember, practice makes perfect!

On the next page, you will find a blind rewrite exercise.

Write your full response to the question we've been using throughout this chapter.

You should time yourself to 20 minutes and try not to look at your notes. Then, compare your response to the sample.

Writing Practice

The charts below show the proportions of consumer expenditure by sector.

Summarize the information by selecting and reporting the main features and make comparisons where relevant.

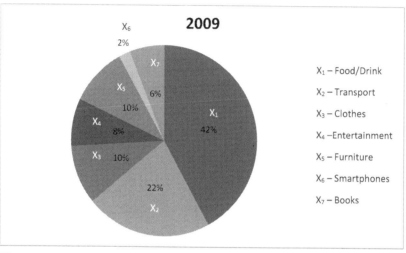

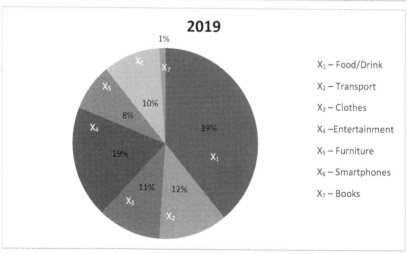

Exercise instructions: Write your response and compare it to the *Sample Response* on the next page.

Write 150-180 words below:

Sample Response

The pie charts depict consumer spending changes in seven different categories in 2009 and 2019.

Overall, the highest proportions were spent on Food and Drink in both years. Entertainment and Smart Phones showed sharp increases in popularity too.

Firstly, consumers spent the most on Food and Drink (42%) and Transport (22%) in 2009. Ten years later, the figures for Food/Drink stayed almost the same at 39%, but Transport plunged sharply to 12%. Meanwhile, spending on Clothes and Furniture did not vary much, hovering between 10-11% and 10-8% respectively in both years.

Some of the biggest changes were seen in Entertainment, Smartphones, and Books. Money spent on Entertainment more than doubled from 8% to 19%, while smartphones showed a similar trend, increasing five-fold over the 10-year period. Finally, books appeared to have lost their appeal, comprising just 1% of the total spending in 2019 compared to 6% ten years earlier.

Chapter 5. Table Descriptions

Reasons for Visiting the London Natural History Museum (in number of people interviewed).

Reason Given	2000	2010	2020
'I came to see specific displays'	52	48	54
Tourism	7	13	22
School Trip	15	22	20
Work	10	11	10

This section will explain the approach to getting a high band score in Task 1, Table Descriptions.

- First and foremost, it is important to remember that Task 1 is a summary question, not an opinion piece or analysis.

- Your 150-word piece should only consist of information directly visible from the table given to you, so there should be no assumptions of any kind.

- Your answer will be graded based on your capability to write about the data in a fluent, structured way and compare information where possible.

- Focus purely on the main features of the data and any necessary and appropriate details.

- Spend only 20 minutes maximum on it; going over will put you at a great disadvantage for task 2.

What should we write about in an IELTS Table Description?

Before you begin your report, you must plan out your content. Start by highlighting the information and comparisons of data shown in the table; here are some general types of trends that you can focus on:

- The highest and lowest numbers

- The overall trend (is it generally ascending or descending)

- The anomaly (the one with the inconsistent trend or showing the most significant change)

The Basic Structure of a Great Table Description

After noting down the important data, you are now ready to plan your response.

Generally, writing task 1 will only need 3 or 4 paragraphs:

Paragraph 1 - Introduction

Paragraph 2 – Overview

Paragraph 3 – 1st highlight and/or comparison

Paragraph 4 – 2nd highlight and/or comparison

Notice again how there is no conclusion above. Since this is a summary of data, no conclusion should be made.

It's best to write in the Present Simple or the Past Simple tense unless the table contains a prediction or forecast, in which case you would use the Future. When choosing either the Past Simple or the Present Simple to describe your table, the important thing is to keep it consistent. If you choose to use the Past Simple, you can't switch to the Present Simple unless you have a good reason. This also applies to any other type of Task 1 in the IELTS Writing exam. Remember that when we respond to the question, we are describing a set of facts rather than telling a creative story.

IELTS Table Exercise 1

Read the following example task.

1. Analyze the question

2. Plan your response.

The table below shows the results of a survey carried out with visitors to the London Natural History Museum.

Summarize the information by selecting and reporting the main features and make comparisons where relevant.

Write at least 150 words.

Reasons for Visiting the London Natural History Museum (in number of people interviewed).

Reason Given	2000	2010	2020
'I came to see specific displays'	52	48	54
Tourism	7	13	22
School Trip	15	22	20
Work	10	11	10

Write a Great Introduction

All you have to do is paraphrase as we've seen in previous chapters, a technique we use to rewrite certain sentences differently without changing the meaning. In Task 1, it is always the introduction sentence to the question combined with the title of the table.

For example, the question above states: "The table below shows the results of a survey carried out with visitors to the London Natural History Museum."

The title of the table is: "Reasons for visiting the London Natural History Museum (in number of people interviewed)."

Now rewrite this in your own words;

....
....
....
....

For instance, we can write:

The table illustrates the outcome of a survey conducted with London Natural History Museum visitors to learn the reasons for their visit.

Write a Great Overview

Jump straight into the obvious information; in this case, the table compares four reasons with the years the survey was taken. Now, highlight the most significant numbers. Look for:

- The highest and lowest numbers

- The overall trend

- The anomaly (the one with the inconsistent trend or showing the most significant change)

- Remember to be general in your overview; don't give specific data.

Now, write your overview in your own words;

....
....
....
....

Here is how you could write your overview for this table:

It (The graphic) compares four reasons for touring the museum in 2000, 2010, and 2020, with the desire 'to see specific displays' proving to be the most popular reason for visiting in all three years. **Meanwhile,** *'Tourism' saw the most significant growth, followed by 'School Trips,' while 'Work' remained relatively unchanged throughout.*

Paragraph 3 - Data highlight 1

The next part should elaborate on the data further; for instance, we can summarize the reason with the most consistent increase across the data or the reason with a near-constant number:

Now write paragraph 3 in your own words;

....
....
....
....

Here is how you could write paragraph 3 for this table:

'Wanting to witness specific displays' presented a slight decrease between 2000 and 2010, going from 52 to 48 as the rest rose, but it grew again in the third interview, ending with 54 people. From 2010 to 2020, 'Work' and 'School trip' dropped by 1 and 2, respectively.

Paragraph 4 - Data highlight 2

Last but not least you can point out the increases and decreases. Make sure not to mention all of them individually but rather in a trend.

Write paragraph 4 in your own words;

....
....
....
....

Here is how you could write paragraph 4 for this table:

Out of the four reasons, 'Work' was the least popular, with minor fluctuations between 10 and 11 across the three interviews, while 'Tourism' showed the most dramatic climb, from 7 in 2000 to 15 in 2010, and ending with 22 in 2020.

IELTS Table Exercise 2

Read the question again and then analyze Sample Response 1 below.

What mistakes can you see?

How would you improve it?

Correct as many things as you can and then check the Suggested Answers on the next page, and Sample Response 2.

The table below shows the results of a survey carried out with visitors to the London Natural History Museum. Summarize the information by selecting and reporting the main features and make comparisons where relevant.

Write at least 150 words.

Reasons for Visiting the London Natural History Museum (in number of people interviewed).

Reason Given	2000	2010	2020
'I came to see specific displays'	52	48	54
Tourism	7	13	22
School Trip	15	22	20
Work	10	11	10

Sample Response (With Errors)

The table shows information about the number of visitors to the London Natural History Museum between 2000 to 2020.

Overall, what stands out from the table is that there was a considerable upward trend of people who visited the museum for tourism.

Looking at the details, 52 visitors chose wanting to see specific displays as their reason in 2000, then the figure went down slightly to around 48 people in 2010. In 2020, the number of visitors wanting to see specific displays rose to 54. By contrast, around 7 visitors chose tourism for visiting the museum in 2000. Next, the figure almost doubled with 13 people in 2010 and then leveled off at 22 visitors in 2020.

Regarding school trip, 15 people chose it as their reason in 2000. There was a significant increase to 22 visitors in 2010 and then leveled off at 20 people in 2020. Looking at work, the figure started at 10 people in 2000, then marginally increased to 11 people in 2020. Lastly, it fell slightly again to 10 visitors in 2020.

Suggested Answers

The table shows information about the number of visitors to the London Natural History Museum <u>between 2000 to 2020.</u> –("**between** X **and** Y" or "**from** X **to** Y")

Overall, <u>what stands out from the table is that</u> - **(this is a waste of words and it makes the report look less professional. It also repeats the word table unnecessarily)** there was a considerable upward trend of people who visited the museum for tourism.

Looking at the details, 52 visitors chose wanting to see specific displays as their reason in 2000, then the <u>figure</u> - **(should be plural)** went down slightly to around 48 people in 2010. In 2020, the number of visitors wanting to see specific displays rose to 54. By contrast, around 7 visitors chose tourism for visiting the museum in 2000. Next, the <u>figure</u> almost doubled with 13 people in 2010 and <u>then leveled off –</u> <u>(Wrong use of "leveled off." Leveled off means it reached a</u> <u>steady rate without change. In this case, there was a change</u> **since it increased to 22)** at 22 visitors in 2020.

<u>Regarding school trip,</u>- **(grammatically incorrect. "School Trip" is a reason given in the questionnaire. It can't be introduced by saying "Regarding" since it is not a topic we are going to discuss; it's a response given by people in a questionnaire.)** 15 people chose it as their reason in 2000. There was a significant increase to 22 visitors in 2010 and <u>then leveled off</u> at 20 people in 2020. Looking at work, the <u>figure</u> started at 10 people in 2000, then marginally increased to 11 people in 2020. Lastly, it fell slightly again to 10 visitors in 2020.

Full Sample Response 2 (Corrected)

Here is what the sample answer looks like together:

The table illustrates the outcome of a survey conducted with London Natural History Museum visitors to learn the reasons for their visit.

The graphic/table compares four reasons for touring the museum in 2000, 2010, and 2020, with the desire 'to see specific displays' proving to be the most popular reason for visiting in all three years. 'Tourism' saw the most significant growth, followed by 'School Trips,' while 'Work' remained relatively unchanged throughout.

'Wanting to witness specific displays' **presented a slight decrease between** 2000 **and** 2010, **going from** 52 to 48 **as the rest rose**, but it grew again in the third interview, ending with 54 people. From 2010 to 2020, 'Work' and 'School trip' dropped by 1 and 2, respectively.

Out of the four reasons, 'Work' was the least popular, with **minor fluctuations** between 10 and 11 across the three interviews, while 'Tourism' **showed the most dramatic climb, from** 7 in 2000 **to** 15 in 2010, and ending with 22 in 2020.

As long as you follow the principles and structure of task 1, your piece should sound cohesive, easy to follow, and easy to understand.

Chapter 6. Mixed Chart Descriptions in IELTS Academic Writing

One of the toughest IELTS writing task 1 questions is the mixed or combined chart question. Most IELTS candidates dread this question because they have no idea how to answer it. This is because most people don't prepare well enough for this type of question.

In a mixed chart question, you will be given two different graphs or images that contain data related to the same main topic.

In this chapter, we will look at a step-by-step strategy to tackle mixed graph IELTS writing questions, and we will use a sample question and a high-scoring model answer to help illustrate these methods.

➤ Analyze the question

➤ Plan out your report structure

➤ Write a good introduction

➤ Write an overview paragraph

➤ Write the main body paragraphs

To show these steps, we will use the following sample question:

The pie chart illustrates the main reason why agricultural land tends to become less productive. The table illustrates the effect of these causes in three European countries between 2002 and 2012.

Select and report the main features, making comparisons where relevant. Write at least 150 words.

Causes of worldwide land Degradation

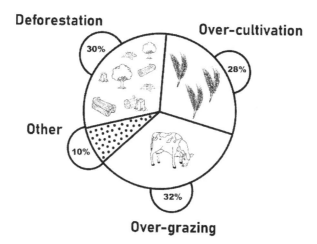

Causes of land degradation by country (2002-2012)

Country	% land degraded by ...			
	deforestaion	over cultivation	Over grazing	Total land degraded
Germany	0.2	3.3	1.5	5%
Italy	9.8	7.7	5.5	23%
Russia	1.7	0	11.3	13%

Analyze

Many students make the mistake of thinking that since they only have 20 minutes for this type of question, they should start writing as soon as possible. However, this is often a costly mistake because you need to do some groundwork to produce a high-scoring report.

The first thing you need to do is extract as much information from the titles of both graphs as possible. Make sure that you note down the different quantities that are being measured and their units of measurement.

It's important to note down the time periods mentioned in both graphs as this will tell you which tense to use when describing the data. You should also be careful because the time periods for each graph may not always be the same.

For example, in our sample question, the pie chart does not relate to any specific time period, meaning that when we describe this data, we will do so using the present tense.

However, the data mentioned in the table is for 2002-2012, meaning that we have to use the past tense when we discuss this data in our report.

A Common Problem with Mixed Graph Questions

A common problem with this type of question is that students often write too much. They try to include as much information as possible for both graphs because they can't decide what to focus on.

Remember, in your report, you only have to discuss the main trends and features of the graph; writing about every detail and change in both graphs will give the examiner the impression that you could not analyze and understand the data and that you have no idea about the main trends and features presented in any of the graphical information. This will negatively affect your Task Achievement score since Task Achievement is related to how well you answered all parts of the question. All writing task 1 report questions ask you to "summarize and report the main features." Therefore, you should not mention minute (unimportant) details in your report.

You should pick about 2 to 3 main features. This will make it easier to develop your main body paragraphs.

You can decide what these main features are by looking at the graph.

Note the extreme data points, like the highest or lowest values.

Comparing and contrasting is one of the important skills that the examiner will be looking out for, so keep an eye out for trends that are either very similar or trends that show contradictory (or inverse) behavior.

You should have a maximum of three main features for each graph; any more would be too confusing and too difficult to explain in only 20 minutes.

By looking at the pie chart in the example, we can see that:

Causes of worldwide land Degradation

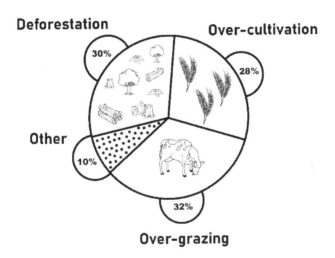

- The pie chart is about the different reasons for the loss of land productivity.

- The quantities are measured in percentages.

- Overgrazing has the highest amount at 32%.

- The other two categories have similar values, with deforestation at 30% and over-cultivation at 28%.

- The category for 'Other' is the lowest at 10%.

- No time periods are mentioned for this pie chart.

By looking at the table, we can see that:

Causes of land degradation by country (2002-2012)

Country	% land degraded by ...			
	deforestaion	over cultivation	Over grazing	Total land degraded
Germany	0.2	3.3	1.5	5%
Italy	9.8	7.7	5.5	23%
Russia	1.7	0	11.3	13%

- The table shows the percentage of agricultural land degraded and the main reasons for this.

- The quantities are measured in percentages.

- Italy had the greatest percentage of land degradation at 23 percent, and the main cause of this was deforestation at 9.8 percent, followed closely by over-cultivation at 7.7 percent.

- Russia had a total of 13 percent of its agricultural land rendered unusable, and the main reason for this was over-grazing at 11.3 percent.

- Germany had the lowest figure at 5 percent, and this was mostly caused by over-cultivation at 3.3 percent.

- The table displays data for the period 2002-2012.

Write a Great Introduction

- You should include a well-thought-out introduction about the type of information present in the report.

- You need to mention the type of quantities being described and their units of measurement.

- You should also make sure that you include information about both types of graphs so that it is clear to the reader that this report is based on more than one piece of graphical information.

- To write an introduction paragraph, you need to paraphrase the information mentioned in the first sentence of the question statement using appropriate synonyms, and this sentence should be about 40 to 50 words long.

      Question Statement: The pie chart illustrates the main reason why agricultural land tends to become less productive. The table illustrates the effect of these causes in three European countries between 2002 and 2012.

      Now rewrite this in your own words;

....

....

Sample Introduction: *The given graphs provide information about the loss of productivity in agricultural lands. To be more specific, the pie chart lists the main reasons for the loss of productivity in agricultural areas, while the table presents the impact in three major countries affected from 2002 to 2012.*

Write a Great Overview Paragraph

In an overview paragraph, you need to mention the most obvious features and trends that can be seen in both graphs. This paragraph should be about two to three sentences at most. Do not let the fact that there are two graphs trick you into adding extra details here.

Now, write your overview in your own words;

Sample Overview: *Overall, the pie chart clearly shows that the greatest cause of land degradation is usually over-grazing. The table identifies that the country with the most severe loss of agricultural productivity was Italy, with significantly higher degradation than Russia. The least affected country was Germany, which experienced relatively low degradation.*

Write the Main Body Paragraphs

- In our main body paragraphs, we will support the information given in our overview with more detail.

- As always, we should write as if the reader has not seen the graphical information and is relying only on our report to understand the trends.

- Therefore, we should use separate paragraphs to describe the data from each graph.

- This will make it easier for the reader to understand the information presented in our report.

Now write paragraph 3 in your own words;

....

....

....

....

Sample Main Body Paragraph 3:

According to what is shown, overgrazing is the most significant reason for agricultural land degradation, with a value of 32%. The other two categories have similar values, with 30% for deforestation and 28% for over-cultivation. The category for other causes is the lowest at 10%.

Now write paragraph 4 in your own words;

....

....

Sample Main Body Paragraph 4:

In 2002-2012, Italy had by far the greatest percentage of land degradation at 23%, and the main cause for this was deforestation at 9.8%, followed closely by over-cultivation at 7.7%. Additionally, Russia had a total of 13% of its agricultural land rendered unusable, and the main reason for this was over-grazing at 11.3%. In comparison, Germany had the lowest levels of degradation at 5%, mostly caused by over-cultivation (3.3%).

Full Sample Response

The given graphs provide information about the loss of productivity in agricultural lands. To be more specific, the pie chart lists the main reasons for the loss of productivity in agricultural areas, while the table presents the impact in three major countries affected from 2002 to 2012.

Overall, the pie chart clearly shows that the greatest cause of land degradation is usually over-grazing. The table identifies that the country with the most severe loss of agricultural productivity was Italy, with significantly higher degradation than Russia. The least affected country was Germany, which experienced relatively low degradation.

According to what is shown, overgrazing is the most significant reason for agricultural land degradation, with a value of 32%. The other two categories have similar values, with 30% for deforestation and 28% for over-cultivation. The category for other causes is the lowest at 10%.

In 2002-2012, Italy had by far the greatest percentage of land degradation at 23%, and the main cause for this was deforestation at 9.8%, followed closely by over-cultivation at 7.7%. Additionally, Russia had a total of 13% of its agricultural land rendered unusable, and the main reason for this was over-grazing at 11.3%. In comparison, Germany had the lowest levels of degradation at 5%, mostly caused by over-cultivation (3.3%).

Mixed Chart Exercise 2

The charts below show the main reasons for study among art students of different ages and the level of satisfaction they reported after they began their new course.

Reasons for study according of student

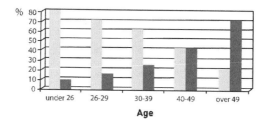

Career progresion
personal interest or passion

Percentage of students by age   who declared themselves to be 'very satisfied' with their choice of course

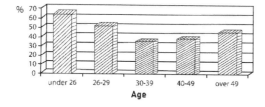

Exercise instructions: Write your response and
compare it to *Full Sample Response 2* on the next page.

Write 150-180 words below:

Sample Response

The first chart **shows** the factors that motivated each student age group to study art, **while** the second one **represents** the percentage of those same groups that were 'very satisfied with their choice.

Overall, **most** younger art students chose this course of study to further their careers, **while** the older students mainly chose art to pursue their personal interests. **Interestingly**, the number of students in the three youngest groups who were very satisfied with the decision **declined** as the age ranges **increased**.

The highest figures for the category of career progression can be seen in the younger age groups, starting at 80% for the under 26-year-olds. **However**, the values **declined gradually** for every age level, with the lowest numbers recorded in the over-49 age group at **roughly** 20%.

The percentage of students who declared themselves 'very satisfied' was also highest in the under-26 age group at **around** 60%. This number **declined steadily** for the other two youngest groups. The least satisfied group overall was the age group between 30 and 39, with **just over** 30%. In **contrast**, satisfaction **increased gradually** for the 40 to 49 and over 49 groups at **around** 30 and 40%, **respectively**.

Chapter 7. Process Descriptions

This chapter outlines the thought process and structure needed to answer an IELTS Process Description question, as well as the elements that need to be included to achieve the best possible band score. It provides a comprehensive overview of the strategic approach to tackle these unique questions, from understanding the prompt and planning your response to the specific language that effectively describes sequential actions and events. We will also explore various examples that demonstrate how to clearly and coherently present a logical sequence, ensuring that your description flows smoothly and adheres to the formal style required by the IELTS exam. Additionally, practical tips and exercises will be offered to enhance your ability to accurately and efficiently convey information, helping you master the skills necessary to excel in this section of the test.

Example Question:

The diagram illustrates how bees produce honey.

Summarize the information by selecting and reporting the main features and make comparisons where relevant.

Write at least 150 words.

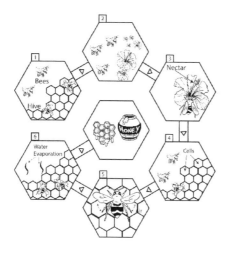

Nectar: A sugary fluid produced by flowers to encourage pollination.
Hive: A dome-shaped or boxlike structure where bees live.
Evaporation: The process of turning from water into vapour.

Step 1- Understand the Process

The first sentence tells us what is shown in the diagram, but we must take time to look at the diagram itself to fully understand what happens in the process.

Remember: we cannot describe something if we do not understand it!

Thought Process:

- The diagram *tells us (**illustrates**)* how bees *make (**produce**)* honey

- The diagram has numbers and arrows, so it is easy to see the beginning and end of the process

- There are not many words on the diagram, so we must use the pictures to help

- There are some words explained underneath the diagram, so they must be important!

Basic Process Outline:

Picture 1 – bees live in a hive

Picture 2 – bees fly around and visit flowers

Picture 3 – bees collect nectar from each flower

Picture 4 – the nectar is left/deposited/transferred into cells inside the hive

Picture 5 – bees flap their wings, which causes/creates movement of air/ air movement

Picture 6 – water evaporates from the nectar

Picture 7 – honey is left behind

What Should We Do?

- Read the question and study the diagram so we know what is happening in the process

- Make a note of the words on the diagram

- Think about our own words and synonyms that we can use.

Step 2- Plan Your Answer

It is important to plan the structure of our writing so that we have included all the elements needed for a Band 9 answer.

Remember: we must structure our writing so that the reader can understand and learn from what we are describing. Imagine the examiner can't see the process diagram and needs your help to understand it.

We need an introduction that tells the reader what we are writing about – We can do this by rewriting and paraphrasing the first sentence of the question using synonyms.

ORIGINAL WORD/PHRASE	POSSIBLE ALTERNATIVE PHRASES/SYNONYMS
The diagram	The picture, illustration, image, graphic
illustrates	shows, explains, demonstrates
how	the way in which the process of
produce	make

- We need to give an overview of the whole process without giving specific details

- We need to write two paragraphs that **select and report** (describe) the main features of the process – We need to decide what the main features are.

Main feature No. 1	Pictures 1, 2 & 3	Bees are outside collecting nectar
Main feature No. 2	Pictures 4, 5, 6 & 7	What happens when the bees return to the hive

Basic Structure

- Think about possible alternative phrases and synonyms to rewrite the first sentence of the question

- Think about how I will describe the whole process

- Identify the main features of the process

- Plan what information my paragraphs will include.

Paragraph 1	Introduction	Rewrite the first sentence of the question
Paragraph 2	Overview	Describe the whole process
Paragraph 3	First main feature	Bees are outside collecting nectar
Paragraph 4	Second main feature	What happens when the bees return to the hive

Step 3- Describe

Follow your plan (**introduction, overview, main features**) to stay focused on the question.

Remember: you only have 20 minutes, so stay focused and stick to your plan.

There are certain things you must include in your writing to make sure you get the best mark you can.

Exercise 1: Writing an Introduction

Write ONE SENTENCE to introduce the process description using the exam question below. Remember to paraphrase as much as possible, and remember to check your paragraph for grammar and vocabulary mistakes at the end.

When you have finished, and you have checked for mistakes, look at the *Answers* section at the end of this chapter.

Exam Question:

You should spend about 20 minutes on this task. The diagram illustrates how bees produce honey. Summarize the information by selecting and reporting the main features, and make comparisons where relevant.

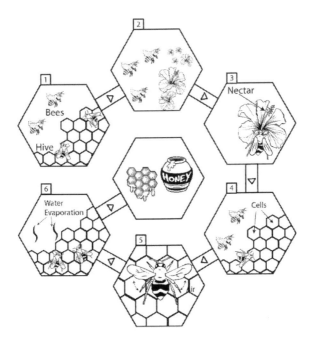

Nectar: A sugary fluid produced by flowers to encourage pollination.
Hive: A dome-shaped or boxlike structure where bees live.
Evaporation: The process of turning from water into vapour.

Write here:

Exercise 2: Writing an Overview

Write a ONE-SENTENCE PARAGRAPH to give an overview of the process description using the same exam question as in Exercise 1.

Remember to paraphrase as much as possible, and remember to check your paragraph for grammar and vocabulary mistakes at the end.

When you have finished, and you have checked for mistakes, look at the Answers section at the end of this chapter.

Write here:

Exercise 3: Writing Body Paragraph 1

Write the FIRST MAIN BODY PARAGRAPH to give details about the process, using the same exam question as in Exercises 1 and 2. Remember to check your paragraph for grammar and vocabulary mistakes at the end.

When you have finished, and you have checked for mistakes, look at the Answers section at the end of this chapter.

Write here:

Exercise 4: Writing Body Paragraph 2

Write the SECOND MAIN BODY PARAGRAPH to give details about the process, using the same exam question as in Exercises 1-3. Remember to check your paragraph for grammar and vocabulary mistakes at the end.

When you have finished, and you have checked for mistakes, look at the Answers section at the end of this chapter.

Write here:

Exercise 5: Grammar & Vocabulary

Read the process description below and fill in the blanks with the missing word or phrase. The sentences are worded DIFFERENTLY to the Samples given in the answers to exercises 1-4.

The illustration explains the process of .... honey in beehives.

Overall, there are seven .... stages in this process, ... the honey bees .... a hive .... the collection and use of the honey.

Firstly, the bees build a dome-shaped or box-like .... in which to live. The hive .... many individually-built units, called cells. Next, the bees leave the hive .... search for flowers. Bees are attracted to flowers by their scent, and they collect nectar, a sticky, sugary substance, from each flower that they visit. This substance is .... to the production of honey.

When the bees return to the hive, the nectar is deposited into the cells. Once this is done, the nectar is cooled down by the movement of air created by the flapping of the bees' wings, ... also causes the nectar to lose its water content. Finally, the honey is left as the product of the whole process and can be enjoyed as a deliciously sweet treat.

Answers

Sample Introductory Sentence

The illustration explains the process of honey production in bee hives.

Sample Overview Sentence

There are seven key stages in this whole process, beginning with the honey bees building a hive and concluding with the collection and use of the honey.

Sample Main Body Paragraph 1

Firstly, the bees build a dome-shaped or box-like structure, called a hive, in which to live. It consists of many individually-built units, called cells. Then, the bees leave the hive in order to search for flowers. They are attracted to flowers by their scent and, as a result, they collect nectar, a sticky, sugary substance, from each flower that they visit. It is this substance that forms the basis of honey production.

Sample Main Body Paragraph 2

When the bees return to the hive, the nectar is deposited into the cells. Next, the nectar is cooled down by the movement of air created by the flapping of the bees' wings. This also causes the nectar to lose its water content. Finally, the honey is left as the product of the whole process and can be enjoyed as a deliciously sweet treat.

Exercise 5: Grammar & Vocabulary

The illustration explains the process of producing honey in beehives.

Overall, there are seven main stages in this process, from the honey bees building a hive to the collection and use of the honey.

Firstly, the bees build a dome-shaped or box-like hive in which to live. The hive contains many individually-built units, called cells. Next, the bees leave the hive to search for flowers. Bees are attracted to flowers by their scent, and they collect nectar, a sticky, sugary substance, from each flower that they visit. This substance is central/crucial/vital/key to the production of honey.

When the bees return to the hive, the nectar is deposited into the cells. Once this is done, the nectar is cooled down by the movement of air created by the flapping of the bees' wings, which also causes the nectar to lose its water content. Finally, the honey is left as the product of the whole process and can be enjoyed as a deliciously sweet treat.

Full Sample Response Version 3

This diagram presents the process by which bees make honey.

There are seven key stages in this process, beginning with the honey bees building a hive and concluding with the collection and use of the honey.

Firstly, the bees build a dome-shaped or box-like structure, called a hive, in which to live. It consists of many individually-built units, called cells. Then, the bees leave the hive to search for flowers. They are attracted to flowers by their scent, and, as a result, they collect nectar, a sticky, sugary substance, from each flower they visit. It is this substance that forms the basis of honey production.

When the bees return to the hive, the nectar is deposited into the cells. Next, the nectar is cooled down by the air movement created by the flapping of the bees' wings, which also causes the nectar cells to lose their water content. Finally, the honey is left as the product of the whole process and can be enjoyed as a deliciously sweet treat.

Extra Language for Process Descriptions

The procedure for... is as follows.

In order to ...the following process takes place.

First of all,...

Then...

After that...

At the next stage...

This is done by...

Finally,...

This completes the procedure.

Chapter 8. Map Descriptions

In the IELTS exam, you might be asked to write a report based on pictorial information such as a process or a map.

A map question usually asks you to describe the changes that happened to an area over a given period of time.

Writing Task 1 Map questions are arguably among the toughest questions to tackle in the IELTS exam. This is mainly because candidates have to use a set of map-related vocabulary that they might not be used to. The main features and changes are not as clear-cut as in the typical graph and chart questions. For these reasons, it's important to go into the exam with a good strategy to help you write a high-scoring response.

Despite being slightly different from the other task 1 question types, the steps to produce a good map description remain the same.

You need to:

Analyze the question

Plan out your report structure

Write a good introduction

Write an overview paragraph

Write the main body paragraphs describing the changes which have taken place.

Analyze The Question.

The question statement will provide you with several useful pieces of information, such as the name of the area that needs to be described and the time periods represented. This will help you decide which tense to use in your report.

You need to study the map and look for features that have disappeared, together with new features. You also need to make note of anything that hasn't changed.

We will use the sample question on the next pages to illustrate these points:

Charmington
1995

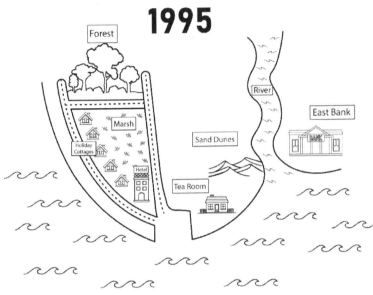

Forest

River

East Bank

Marsh

Sand Dunes

Holiday Cottages

Hotel

Tea Room

Lake

2025

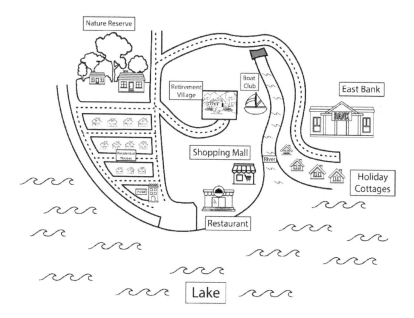

Notes:

- This map shows the town of Charmington

- There are two time periods, 1995 (in the past) and 2025 (in the future)

    New features in 2025:

    Nature reserve

    Residential Housing

A boat club

A restaurant

A retirement village

A shopping mall.

Holiday cottages (moved)

Features that remain the same:

The hotel

Write A Great Introduction

The introduction paragraph should give the reader an idea about which area is being discussed and the relevant time period. To write a good introductory paragraph, you just need to paraphrase the first statement in the question.

Question Statement: The map below shows the town of Charmington in 1995 and 2025.

Now rewrite this in your own words;

....

....

....

....

Sample Introduction: *The map represents the town of Charmington as it was in 1995 and how it is predicted to look in 2025.*

Write a Great Overview Paragraph

In this paragraph, you must discuss the overall changes in the maps without mentioning too many specific details.

Now, write an overview in your own words;

....
....
....
....

Sample Overview: *The town used to be much less built up, and by 2025, new developments will significantly change the landscape. The most significant changes are that the town will have ample accommodation for residents as well as a brand-new shopping mall, and there will be numerous tourist-friendly amenities.*

Write The Main Body Paragraphs

In the main body paragraphs, you need to provide details about the changes to the map that you noted when analyzing the question. Many students find it easier to organize map information according to time and period. You can dedicate a separate paragraph for each time period to do this.

Note: You can organize it differently, where you compare each feature side by side, but for this example, we will organize it by time period.

Now write 2-3 body paragraphs in your own words;

Sample Main Body Paragraphs:

In 1995, most of Charmington was undeveloped, and there were just a few holiday cottages and a hotel on the western side, as well as a small tearoom near the dunes in the south and a bank on the riverfront.

However, the map for 2025 shows that some radical changes are planned for the town. To the northwest of Charmington, the forest will be turned into a nature reserve. Additionally, the nearby marsh area will be developed into residential housing units, and the holiday cottages will be demolished and rebuilt, facing the lake next to the East Bank.

A new town center will be built to include several new facilities such as a boat club on the riverfront, a retirement village, and a shopping mall, built where the dunes used to be. Meanwhile, the small tearoom next to the dunes will be upgraded to a restaurant. The only features of the map to remain the same are the hotel in the southeast of the town and the East Bank.

Exercise: Cutting Out Unnecessary Words

The following full sample response is too long.

How can we make it shorter to make our writing more efficient?

The map represents the town of Charmington as it was in 1995 and how it is predicted to look in 2025.

The town used to be much less built up, and by 2025, new developments will significantly change the landscape. The most significant changes are that the town will have ample accommodation for residents as well as a brand-new shopping mall, and there will be numerous tourist-friendly amenities.

In 1995, most of Charmington was undeveloped, and there were just a few holiday cottages and a hotel on the western side, as well as a small tearoom near the dunes in the south and a bank on the riverfront.

However, the map for 2025 shows that some radical changes are planned for the town. To the northwest of Charmington, the forest will be turned into a nature reserve. Additionally, the nearby marsh area will be developed into residential housing units, and the holiday cottages will be demolished and rebuilt, facing the lake next to the East Bank.

A new town center will be built to include several new facilities such as a boat club on the riverfront, a retirement village, and a shopping mall, built where the dunes used to be. Meanwhile, the small tearoom next to the dunes will be upgraded to a restaurant. The only features of the map to remain the same are the hotel in the southeast of the town and the East Bank.

Suggested Answer

The map represents the town of Charmington as it was in 1995 and how it is predicted to look in 2025.

The town used to be much less built up, and by 2025, new developments will significantly change the landscape. ~~The most significant changes are that~~ **Charmington** will have ample accommodation for residents, ~~as well as~~ a brand-new shopping mall, and ~~there will be~~ numerous tourist-friendly amenities.

In 1995 most of Charmington was undeveloped, ~~and there were~~ **with** just a few holiday cottages and a hotel on the western side, ~~as well as~~ a small tearoom near the dunes in the south, and a bank on the riverfront.

However, the map for 2025 shows ~~that~~ some radical changes ~~are planned for the town~~. To the northwest of Charmington, the forest will be turned into a nature reserve. Additionally, the nearby marsh area will ~~be developed into~~ **become** residential housing units, and the holiday cottages will be ~~demolished and rebuilt facing~~ **moved near** the lake next to the East Bank.

A new town center will be built to include ~~several new facilities such as~~ a boat club on the riverfront, a retirement village, and a shopping mall, ~~built~~ where the dunes used to be. Meanwhile, the small tearoom next to the dunes will be upgraded to a restaurant. ~~The only features of the map to remain the same are the hotel in the southeast of the town and the East Bank.~~ **The hotel in the southeast and the East Bank will remain untouched.**

Map Vocabulary

One of the main problems that students face when writing a description for a map is that they do not use the proper vocabulary related to maps and directions. You must familiarize yourself with these types of words and their usage.

Here are some words and phrases that are useful for a map description:

north

south

east

west

north-east

northwest

southeast

south-west

to the left

to the right

seafront

lakefront

riverfront

nearby

adjacent

besides

between

in front of

behind

radical changes

minor changes

Remember, the best way to familiarize yourself with these new words is to practice using them!

- IELTS GENERAL WRITING PART 1 -

Length: 60 minutes

General Writing Test

Task	Word count	Advised Timing	Task description
1	150	20 mins	The candidate is presented with a situation and is asked to write a letter requesting information, or explaining an issue. The letter may be personal, semi-formal or formal in style.
2	250	40 mins	Presenting arguments and opinions in a discursive essay about a topical issue.

Source: IELTS.org

TIP: The exam says to write a 'minimum of 150/250 words, but don't write much more. Aim for 10 or 20 words more at the most.

The Writing component of the IELTS General includes two tasks. Topics are of general interest to and suitable for candidates entering work and postgraduate studies or seeking professional registration.

Task 1

You will be presented with a problem or an issue and asked to describe, summarize, or explain the information in your own words. You may be asked to write a letter of application, a letter of recommendation, a letter concerning accommodation, or a letter of complaint, among other possibilities.

Task 2

You will be asked to write an essay in response to a point of view, argument, or problem. Responses to both tasks must be formal.

Chapter 9. Formal Letters & Emails for IELTS Writing General Training

In this section, we will examine the formal letter tasks in the IELTS General Training exam.

Firstly, we will practice identifying key information in the question. Next, we will suggest ways to organize formal letters, and then we will look at the kind of language you should be using. Finally, we practice functional language, grammar, and vocabulary, which are essential and will help you gain lots of marks in the exam.

We will examine two formal letter and email types: the letter of reference and the application letter. These aren't the only types of standard letters or emails you might be asked to write about in the exam, but they will serve as perfect examples here.

Letter of Reference

In this type of formal letter, you're asked to provide a reference for a colleague or friend to a prospective employer or educational institution.

You may find it helpful to note down useful expressions which you can include,

Some Useful Language for this type of letter or email

I have known X for ….

I am confident that ….

I have no hesitation in recommending him ….

X is sociable, reliable, self-confident, outgoing

X possesses a thorough grounding in …

stand him in good stead

as is shown by the fact that …

As you may know, your writing will be assessed in terms of:

Task Achievement

Coherence and Cohesion

Lexical Resource

Grammatical Range and Accuracy

Including all the relevant content in your letter and presenting it clearly will contribute hugely towards your scoring well, as the target reader will be fully informed.

Candidates often lose marks in the exam, either because they have included irrelevant information, they've forgotten to include something important or they misinterpreted the question.

Here is a typical example of a formal letter question. We will practice identifying key content to avoid losing marks. We'll work through the task chronologically.

Read the example and answer the following question.

1. What is the first key piece of information you need to refer to in your answer?

A friend of yours is applying for a job in a popular shop as a retail shop assistant for English-speaking tourists visiting your city. The shop has asked you to provide a character reference for your friend.

The reference should indicate

how long you have known each other.

It must include a detailed description of the person's character and the reason why he or she would be suitable for the job.

Write at least 150 words.

This seems like an obvious question, but it's vital to understand that <u>they ask you to write a reference</u>. Firstly, this indicates that we need to be thinking about a formal register, and it also helps us start the letter.

For example:

"To whom it may concern,

Mary and I have been working together at J&J Retail for ten years.

.............."

2. What is the next vital information?

We need to pay attention to the type of job we are writing the reference for. The job, in this case, is a retail assistant for a popular shop. It is important to remember that the information we provide must be relevant to this position.

3. What qualities or skills does a suitable candidate for almost any job need to have?

You can use the following ideas for any job reference.

i. Personal and social skills (people skills/interpersonal abilities): The successful candidate will need to have good personal and social skills, so we must emphasize the person's personal and social skills in the context of their application.

ii. English language skills: we must emphasize his or her English language skills, as all jobs that you will be asked to write references for in this exam will require the candidate to speak good English to communicate with customers, clients, tourists, guests, etc.....

iii. Time-management ability is another skill that every person needs for a job, so regardless of the job they present you with, you can talk about this.

4. So what's next?

Previous experience. We need to mention any relevant work the person has done in the past that will support their application. Again, we could link this with the earlier part about their people skills or their time-management skills.

We need to show the person is suitable for the post, but this doesn't necessarily need to be in a separate paragraph. You can write about their experience in the same section while you describe their character and skills.

Alternatively, it could be something you include at the end of the letter, but either way, you always need to emphasise the person's suitability for the post.

Organization (Reference and Application):

Reread the example and answer the following questions.

1. How many paragraphs would you have?

2. Which sections would deal with which issues?

Example Question

A friend of yours is applying for a job in a popular shop as a retail shop assistant for English-speaking tourists visiting your city. The shop has asked you to provide a character reference for your friend.

The reference should indicate

• how long you have known each other.

• It must include a detailed description of the person's character

• the reason why he or she would be suitable for the job.

Write at least 150 words.

One idea is to organize this around two or three content paragraphs along with an opening and closing paragraph, so four or five paragraphs in total.

Step-by-Step Plan:

Paragraph 1

The first paragraph deals with our reason for writing. In this case, our motivation is to write a reference for a friend (or in the letter of application to apply for something). In a letter of reference or a letter of application, the first main content paragraph usually outlines the person's skills and experience, perhaps including any relevant qualifications they might have.

Paragraph 2

Then, we could move on to look at the person's character and their personal qualities.

We could deal with our friend's suitability for the post in these two paragraphs if we wanted to, or we could choose to have a third content paragraph where we emphasise the person's strengths once again.

Finally, we would end the letter with a closing remark such as: *"Please do not hesitate to contact me if you have any questions. "*

Organizing your paragraphs logically like this would make the letter coherent overall. It would give the reader a visual guide to your organization, especially if you leave a line of space between each paragraph. It would also help you deal with the main sections of the letter in a logical order.

Expressing Ideas

But what about how you express ideas within paragraphs? How can you link ideas in and between sentences? Let's look at some of the ways you can do this.

Linking Words:

The first method is linking words that you've probably used in your writing for a while. Words or expressions like *firstly* or *in addition, for instance,* enable you to link ideas simply and effectively.

Discourse Markers:

The assessment criteria often refer to discourse markers. These are just slightly higher-level linking words or expressions such as *moreover, furthermore,* or *by way of example.*

Exercise

Look at the gaps in the sample answer below:

Where could you use these linking words and discourse markers to complete the text? You will not need to sue all of them.

Firstly, in addition, for instance, moreover, furthermore, or by way of example.

To whom it may concern,

Mary and I worked together at J&J Retail for ten years.

It is my pleasure to recommend her for the position of Shop Assistant.

1....................., Mary is a self-confident and outgoing person who finds it easy to relate to people from all kinds of backgrounds.

During her time at J&J Retail, Mary proved to be friendly, communicative, hard-working, and excellent at managing her time. 2....................., Mary is the kind of person who works well with others, as she displays excellent sensitivity and sympathy. She was always willing to contribute and help her colleagues. 3.................. at J&J Retail, she was popular and fully committed to the organization's objectives.

4.................. at J&J Retail, Mary demonstrated excellent English language skills in dealing with English-speaking customers daily. She passed her English exams around six months ago and has a keen interest in fashion, which I am sure will stand her in good stead when she is helping customers in English.

I recommend Mary without reservation — she would be an excellent asset to your company.

Please do not hesitate to contact me if you have any questions.

Sincerely,

Joe Bloggs

Sample Answer (Letter of Reference):

To whom it may concern,

Mary and I worked together at J&J Retail for ten years.

It is my pleasure to recommend her for the position of Shop Assistant.

Firstly, Mary is a self-confident and outgoing person who finds it easy to relate to people from all kinds of backgrounds.

During her time at J&J Retail, Mary proved to be friendly, communicative, hard-working, and excellent at managing her time. In addition, Mary is the kind of person who works well with others, as she displays excellent sensitivity and sympathy. She was always willing to contribute and help her colleagues. Moreover, (Furthermore) at J&J Retail, she was popular and fully committed to the organization's objectives.

By way of example, (For instance) at J&J Retail, Mary demonstrated excellent English language skills in dealing with English-speaking customers daily. She passed her English exams around six months ago and has a keen interest in fashion, which I am sure will stand her in good stead when she is helping customers in English.

I recommend Mary without reservation — she would be an excellent asset to your company.

Please do not hesitate to contact me if you have any questions.

Sincerely,

Your Name and Surname

(Word count: 197)

Notes: Well done if you answered correctly, but be careful when you write, as there is always the danger that you can overuse devices like these. This makes your writing seem unnatural and demonstrates to the examiner that you do not understand how to use them.

To avoid this issue, let's look at some other cohesive devices you can use to help you organize your ideas.

Reference pronouns: Reference pronouns like *this, that, they or it is* commonly used to refer back to something or someone recently mentioned.

Relative clauses: Relative clauses can be used to give added information to a statement, and they allow you to link ideas together in well-formed sentences.

Substitution: Other forms of cohesive devices include things like substitution. This is where you use a synonym, for example, to refer backwards or forwards to a connecting point in the text.

E.g., Replacing a verb phrase:

The management team at J & J Retail was delighted with Mary, and so were the rest of the staff (and the rest of the staff were also very happy with her).

Using paragraphs and a variety of cohesive devices effectively will help you score well in the "Coherence and Cohesion" and "Task achievement" parts of the assessment criteria. **Tip:** When you're reading, make a point of looking out for cohesive devices like those we've looked at in this section.

Letter of Application

In this type of formal letter, you're asked to write a formal letter or email applying for a job, accommodation, or place on a course. Again, the recipient of this letter is a prospective employer or educational institution.

Cover letters, sometimes called letters of application, are crucial parts of your application, whether you're a university student or a candidate looking for a job. While there are virtually no limits to the different designs you can use for your letter of application, there are some general guidelines you will want to apply to make sure it is appropriate for the exam. It is, first, essential to make sure your cover letter has an excellent appearance in terms of both structure and language.

Ensure you learn the name of the person or organization you're writing if they appear in the instructions. The name must always be spelled correctly.

The next thing you want to do is to demonstrate your qualifications for the job. It is best to write two powerful sentences explaining why you have the necessary skills to perform the job you are interested in. After this, you will want to let the potential employer know that your resume is enclosed. It is also essential to make sure you don't end the letter incorrectly.

Sample Task

You see this advertisement in an international student magazine.

<u>Write an application to become a volunteer.</u>

Volunteers needed

We are looking for volunteers to help out at a famous international sporting event. We're looking for friendly, respectful people with good language skills, good team skills, and a 'can-do' attitude. We need people to welcome delegates, provide customer service, and solve problems.

If you think you have what it takes, apply now.

You should write at least 150 words.

Spend around 20 minutes on this part.

Where to Start

The first key piece of information in a letter of application is the fact you've seen the advertisement and where you saw it. This will be the perfect way to start the letter.

Remember that you also need to confirm which position you're applying for. This exam is designed to be as realistic as possible, but there may be more than one position in real life. If you didn't mention the specific job, the reader would not be fully informed.

For example:

Dear Sir or Madam,

I am writing to apply for the Volunteer position advertised in the International Student Magazine.

Language Skills

In this example, the international sporting event will give you a chance to emphasize your language skills, such as your ability to speak English fluently.

As with the letter of reference, language skills are something you can and should always mention in a letter of application in the IELTS General exam. All positions advertised will require the candidate to speak or write in English.

Suitability for the job

You need to explain your suitability for the job. The question will sometimes state what the required skills or knowledge are, but typically you'll have to include your experience, your qualifications, if any, and personal qualities.

Finally, it would be a good idea to point out that you're available for an interview and perhaps to state any times when you're not available. If you cover all these points in your answer, logically, persuasively, and in an appropriate format, you should score well in terms of content and communicative achievement.

Full Sample Response (Letter of Application)

Dear Mr./Mrs./Miss/Ms. [Hiring manager name – "Dear Sir or Madam" if name or gender are unknown]

I wish to apply for the role of [Volunteer] advertised in the [International Student Magazine]. Please find enclosed my CV for your consideration.

As you can see from my attached CV, I have over [time period, e.g., five years] experience in [e.g., volunteering or customer service], and I believe the knowledge and skills built up during this time make me the perfect candidate for this position. I am also keen to keep improving my English, as this is not only a hobby but also a real need.

In my current role as a [job title] at [employer name], I have been responsible for [e.g., a 5% increase in revenue], which when coupled with my enthusiasm and dedication [insert skills relevant to the role – usually found in the job description], has helped the business to [measure of success].

I am confident that I can bring this level of success to your organization and help [company name] build upon its reputation as an outstanding company. With my previous experience and expertise, I believe my contribution will have an immediate impact on the business.

Thank you for your time and consideration.

I look forward to meeting with you to discuss my application further.

Yours sincerely/Yours faithfully,

[Your name]

(Word Count 222)

Formal Letter of Complaint

Organization & Essential Language:

As the title suggests, in this section, we will focus on the features of the organization.

In the last section, we looked at two common types of formal letters, which often appear in the exam: the letter of reference and the letter of application. As previously mentioned, both of these tasks are very similar in structure and ideas. In this section, we will use a different example to see the slightly different tone and style required in each type of letter.

Up until now, we have concentrated on spotting the critical content. The essential content is the information we need to respond to in our letter. If you haven't done this yet, stop for a second and note the key points in the letter of reference and the letter of application.

As we saw in the previous section, we need to respond to all of these critical points in our letter to score well in the exam.

Your overall organization of the piece of writing is vital. This includes using logical paragraphs, for example, and the precise organization of ideas within paragraphs. You do this by using linking words, discourse markers, and other devices. The examples in the previous section show you exactly how to organize your letter of reference and letter of application. Still, they do not show you how to organize other types of letters.

This section will look at paragraphing a letter of complaint and at these additional organizational features.

Read the letter of complaint task below and answer the following question:

How would you organize the paragraphs in your letter if you were answering this question? Think about how you might organize the underlined points into logical, coherent paragraphs.

Exercise: Formal Letter of Complaint

Read this extract from a letter you have recently sent to a friend:

".... I forgot to say, don't go to Dino's Bar for your birthday. We went there last night - the service was awful; the food was cold, and it was so expensive for such a bad meal! I complained to a member of staff, but he asked me to put it in writing ..."

Write your letter of complaint to the manager of Dino´s bar

In your letter:

- Introduce yourself

- Explain the situation

- Say what action you would like the company to take

Write at least 150 words.

Question to think about:

How many paragraphs would you have, and which power graphs would deal with which issues?

There are several ways to approach this letter, but one suggestion is to organize it around four content paragraphs, one for each problem and one at the end for suggestions.

The answer to this question can be planned and organized as follows:

The letter can be divided into four paragraphs:

1. Formal "hello" and state the general problem, saying why you went to Dino´s in this case and that you are dissatisfied. State problem 1 (the service was awful)

2. Detailed explanation of problem 2 (the food was cold)

3. Problem 3: the price was high

4. Conclusion: What do you want Dino´s to do? Offer some suggestions for improvement here.

A bit more on each paragraph:

OK, so the first paragraph is going to deal with your reason for writing. In a letter of complaint, the first main content paragraph is used to outline the problem, say why you went to the business you are complaining about, and make sure you say that you are dissatisfied.

Then, we could look at the specific details of the problem, using appropriate adjectives.

Finally, in the last paragraph, we could offer some suggestions or recommendations to improve the business. You can use language such as:

I must insist that you…

I must urge you to…

Essential Language for a Letter of Complaint

I am writing to complain about…

I would like to express my dissatisfaction with …

I am writing to express my concern about the….

I must complain in writing about…

I feel I must complain to you about…

I wish to complain in the strongest terms about…

I am writing to inform you of an apparent error in your records…

Paraphrasing Exercise

Example:

0) Basic Problem: "I want to complain about the lousy service in the restaurant."

ii. Key Language: I would like to express my dissatisfaction with ...

iii, Key Word you must use: POOR (Bad is too informal, so we can use poor instead)

iv. Final Product: "I would like to express my dissatisfaction with the poor standard of service in the restaurant."

Now try to complete the process using the following language:

1)

i. Basic problem: "The cinema is far away from everything."

ii. Key Phrase: I wish to complain in the strongest terms about...

iii. Key Word: ACCESSIBILITY

....
....
....

2)

i. Basic problem: "During my course, there were too many students in the class."

ii. Key Phrase: I am writing to express my concern about the....

iii. Key Word: NUMBER

....
....
....

Answers:

1) I wish to complain in the strongest terms about the accessibility of the cinema.

2) I am writing to express my concern about the number of students in the class during my course

Topic-Specific Phrases

- *Poor standard of service/slow service*

- *I am asking for/I would like to request a replacement*

- *No accommodation/Travel delays/Rather rude staff*

- *Badly scratched/dented wrapping/packaging*

- *To claim/demand for a refund*

- *I am returning ... to you for correction of the fault/for inspection/repair/servicing*

- *Defective/faulty goods/defective item/machine*

- *The... may need replacing*

- *To restore an item to full working order...*

- *I am enclosing the broken radio in this package; please send me a replacement.*

- *You said that ... I feel sure there must be some mistake as I am sure that...*

Ending the letter

- *I do not usually complain, but, as an old customer, I hope you will be interested in my comments.*

- *We look forward to dealing with this matter without delay.*

- *I feel that your company should consider an appropriate refund.*

- *I would be grateful if you would send me a complete refund as soon as possible*

- *We feel there must be some explanation for (this delay) and expect your prompt reply.*

- *Will you please look into this matter and let us know the reason for ...*

- *Thank you for your assistance.*

- *I look forward to hearing from you at your earliest convenience.*

- *I am returning the damaged goods/items... and shall be glad if you will replace them.*

- *Please look into this matter at once and let me know the delay.*

- *Please recheck your records.*

- *Thank you for your cooperation in correcting this detail...*

- *I wish to draw your attention to...*

- *I would suggest that...*

- *I suggest that immediate steps be taken.*

- *I want to complain about...*

- *I look forward to a prompt reply and hope that you will take into consideration...*

- *I am dissatisfied with...*

Exercise: Analyzing a Sample Letter of Complaint

Objective: Enhance understanding of effective language use and structural elements in a letter of complaint for the IELTS exam.

Instructions:

➤ Read the sample letter of complaint provided.

➤ Complete the tasks below that focus on the language and structure used in the letter.

Dear Sir/Madam,

I would like to express my dissatisfaction with the poor standard of service we received during our recent visit to Dino's Bar. Firstly, the staff were generally quite rude and unhelpful, they seemed to lack basic food knowledge, and they did not seem interested in the job. For instance, none of them could offer any advice to me on choosing a dish.

A further cause for complaint was that the food was cold when it arrived at our table. I understand that it was a busy night, but we booked the table and the menus the day before, so I feel that they should have been ready.

Finally, not only did we receive substandard food and unfriendly, unhelpful service, but we were also charged full price for our meals after we complained. In my opinion, the prices seem to be very expensive for the quality of the food and the service provided.

I do not usually complain, but as a loyal customer, I hope you will be interested in my comments. Perhaps it would be appropriate to offer some training courses to the staff at Dino's Bar, to avoid this from happening again. I feel that customer service was a big issue, as was the quality of the food. If these two problems were fixed, then the price might not be such an issue in the future, as customers would be happy to pay a little more for a better experience. I hope you will take these points into consideration.

I look forward to your reply.

Yours faithfully,

Name and Surname

Tasks:

Task 1: Identify and list any phrases used to politely express dissatisfaction. Discuss how these phrases can be altered or used in different complaint scenarios.

Task 2: Examine how the writer structures their complaints. Note the sequence and how each point is introduced. Why do you think the writer structured their points in this way?

Task 3: Look at the suggestions for resolution provided by the writer. Why is it effective to include such suggestions in a complaint letter?

Task 4: Write a concluding sentence that could be used in a similar complaint letter, reflecting hope for a positive response while remaining firm and clear about the dissatisfaction.

Task 5: Create a new complaint based on a different scenario (e.g., a defective product purchased online) using the language and structure observed in the sample letter.

Answer Key for Analyzing a Sample Letter of Complaint

Task 1: Phrases to Express Dissatisfaction

Phrases Identified:

"I would like to express my dissatisfaction with..."

"A further cause for complaint was..."

"I do not usually complain, but..."

Discussion: These phrases are polite yet clearly convey dissatisfaction. They can be adapted for other scenarios, like "I must express my dissatisfaction with the product/service I received" or "Another reason for my disappointment is...".

Task 2: Structure of Complaints

Structure Notes:

1. Introduction of the complaint about service.
2. Details about specific issues (rudeness, lack of knowledge, lack of interest).
3. Additional complaint about the food being cold.
4. The pricing issue was addressed last as it ties into the overall experience.

Reasoning: This structure allows the writer to build the case logically, starting from the most direct interaction (service), moving to product issues (food quality), and ending with pricing. It helps clarify that the service and product issues justify dissatisfaction with the price.

Task 3: Suggestions for Resolution

Effectiveness: Including suggestions such as offering training for staff shows the writer's constructive approach and willingness to help improve the service, rather than just criticizing. It positions the writer as reasonable and invested in future improvements.

Task 4: Sample Concluding Sentence

"I trust that you will address these issues promptly, not only to resolve my concerns but to improve the experience for all your customers."

Structure Rules for Formal Letters & Emails in IELTS General Training

Greeting

Name unknown: *Dear Sir/Madam,*

Name known: *Dear Mr..../ Dear Mrs.... / Dear Ms..+* *surname*

Reason for writing

I am writing to ... I am writing concerning...

I am writing on behalf of ...

Asking questions

I would be grateful if ... I wonder if you could ....

Could you ...?

Referring to someone else's letter /points

As you stated in your letter, ...   Regarding .../ Concerning ...

With regard to ....

Finishing the letter

If you require any further information, please do not hesitate to contact me.

I look forward to hearing from you.

Signing

If Dear + name = Yours sincerely,

If Dear Sir/ Madam = Yours faithfully

Your first name + surname must be written clearly under your signature.

Language Practice: Formal Letters & Emails

Letters can be anything from very formal to very informal. The IELTS General Writing paper will never ask you to write a specialized business or legal letter requiring a professional knowledge of business words, structures, and expressions. However, they might ask you to write a formal, semi-formal, or informal email or letter.

In this section of the chapter, we will focus on your use of language and, in particular, your ability to create a formal register. This will help you do well in two of the assessment criteria: Language, by using a range of formal vocabulary and grammatical structures, and communicative achievement, by creating an appropriate formal tone that has a positive effect on the reader. We will identify some of the features of formal English that we often find in formal letters.

At the end of this section, you will find a list of useful formal-informal equivalents. This list will save you a lot of time in your preparation for the exam. For example, in a letter of complaint: "I was rather disappointed" is a formal way of saying, "I was furious" or "I was furious." See how many more formal and informal equivalent items you can learn next.

Exercise: Sentence Transformations

Transform the informal or semi-formal version of each phrase from a letter of complaint into a formal style. You can make small changes to the sentences' content if you think it´s necessary, and you can use a dictionary.

Example: *I thought I'd write = I am writing*

a. state of the playground =

b. I have noticed loads of rubbish =

c. I reckon =

d. The teacher I'm talking about =

e. On top of this =

f. a load of problems =

g. You could =

h. stop =

i. What's more =

j. better =

k. To finish =

l. I´m looking forward to hearing from you =

Answers:

a. state of the playground = condition of the playground

b. I have noticed loads of rubbish = There is a great deal of litter

c. I reckon = It is my opinion that…

d. The teacher I'm talking about = The teacher in question OR The teacher I am referring to.

e. On top of this = Furthermore

f. a load of problems = several problems

g. You could = it may be possible for you

h. stop = prevent

i. What's more = In addition,

j. better = more suitable OR more adequate

k. To finish = In conclusion,

l. I´m looking forward to hearing from you = I look forward to your reply, OR I look forward to hearing from you

Exercise: Key Words

Now, here are some full sentences from formal letters.

Complete the sentences using only one word.

a. I am writing in .... to your job advertisement in the ABC newspaper

b. I would like to .... for the position of translator.

c. I am .... to come for an interview at any time convenient to you.

d. I would be .... if you could send me further information regarding the position.

e. Please find my CV ....

f. I would like to express my .... with the poor standard of service we received during our recent visit to your cinema.

g. For ...., none of them could offer any advice to me on choosing a dish.

h. Finally, not only .... we receive substandard food and unfriendly, unhelpful service, but we were also charged full price for our meals after we complained.

i. I look forward ....

Answers

a. I am writing in reply/response to your job advertisement in the ABC newspaper

b. I would like to apply for the position of translator.

c. I am available/ able to come for an interview at any time convenient to you.

d. I would be grateful if you could send me further information regarding the position.

e. Please find my CV attached (email)/ enclosed (letter).

f. I would like to express my dissatisfaction with the poor standard of service we received during our recent visit to your cinema.

g. For instance, none of them could offer any advice to me on choosing a dish.

h. Finally, not only did we receive substandard food and unfriendly, unhelpful service, but we were also charged full price for our meals after we complained.

i. I look forward to your reply.

The Passive Voice

Okay, the next example is one where the passive has been used instead of an active form. This is a common feature of formal writing but should not be overused. In real life (business and university included), you should try to avoid the passive, as it needlessly complicates sentences. However, in the IELTS exam, you can use it once or twice to demonstrate versatility to the examiners.

This sentence is an example of how we might structure a sentence formally.

Informal: *"The waiter did offer us another dish, but when it arrived, it was cold again."*

Formal: *"Although we were offered an alternative dish when it was delivered to the table, it was cold again."*

Notice two clauses in the informal version are joined by *but* whereas in the formal version, the two clauses have been reversed and *but* is replaced with *although* which starts the sentence. This is a more formal way of saying the same thing.

Within the formal sentence, *"Although we were offered an alternative dish when it was delivered to the table, it was cold again,"* there are further examples of vocabulary that has been made more formal. For example, an *alternative dish* is a more formal way of saying *another dish*.

As we saw above, phrasal verbs are most typical of informal letters —although there are some that have no more formal equivalents and are common in all types of letters (*look forward to*, for example). However, most phrasal verbs do have formal equivalents, and these would be preferred in most formal letters, whereas the formal equivalents would be very rarely used in an informal letter.

6 Quick Rules of Formal VS Informal

1. We tend to understate our feelings and say *I was rather disappointed,* or *I was somewhat surprised* instead of saying how we really felt.

2. For the same reason, we do not use exclamation marks.

3. We often use the passive to emphasize the action when the person is of less importance

4. We avoid contractions in formal letters.

5. We use formal equivalence of idiomatic language and phrasal verbs

6. Particular sentence structures can be used to create a formal tone. Inversion is one example of this *"Although we were offered an alternative dish when it was delivered to the table, it was cold again."*

Exercise: Rewriting

Rewrite the following sentences using formal equivalents for the phrasal verbs. Use a dictionary if necessary. You might need to make other changes to the structures.

1) I'm so chuffed that you've been talked into coming to the meeting.

....

....

2) The football club's facilities have been done up, so this should make our performances better.

....

....

3) As our town is quite cut off, perhaps we could arrange for you to be put up in a hotel in the city for a few days.

....

....

4) We will make up for the inconvenience of having to wait for so long.

....

....

Answers:

1) I am thrilled that you have been convinced to attend the meeting.

2) The football club's facilities have been refurbished, which should improve our performances.

3) As our town is relatively isolated, we could arrange hotel accommodation in the city for a few days.

4) We will compensate you for the inconvenience of having to wait for so long.

Chapter 10. Informal Letters & Emails

Example Task

An English-speaking friend is visiting your region for a couple of weeks during his holidays and has written to you to ask for several recommendations.

Write a letter to your friend.

In your letter, you should:

• offer to help find accommodation

• advise about things to do

• provide information about what clothes to bring.

In this type of task, you should begin your letter as follows:

Dear ... your friend's name.

A few things to keep in mind.

• You have about 20 minutes to write this.

• You should have at least 150 words. Aim for about 180 (a little bit more, but don't go too long- If you're over 240 words, you've written much more than you need to.)

Let's start with the general idea of what you're trying to do, what you're trying to accomplish.

Tone

'The tone' of the letter means how your letter sounds or the overall feeling it gives the reader. It should be very relaxed and very informal; this is what the examiners are looking for.

For example: if you're writing to your friend, write it as though you were speaking to your friend; very casual.

You can start with:

Dear- Hello- Hi and then the person´s first name, never their surname.

You shouldn´t use *Mr., Mrs., Dr.*

Do not put first and last names because you do not address your friends or family members by their first and last names in real life.

Contractions

Now contractions are suitable. So, in terms of how you're going to use *I've, it's, don't*, etc... In a formal letter, you say *do not,* whereas in an informal letter, you say *don't.*

Slang & idioms

Not only are slang and idioms okay now, but they're recommended because they demonstrate that you can adapt your language to different contexts. When you speak with your friends, you usually use very casual language, including slang and idioms.

Nevertheless, remember it has to be natural, so don't be too heavy on the slang or the idioms. One or two here and there are great, but it becomes unnatural if you overuse them, and the examiners may penalize you for it.

Note that you can use idioms in your formal letter as well, but very carefully and selectively, and it has to be very appropriate, so it´s generally not recommended.

Here are some examples of informal language you can use for different types of informal emails and letters in English.

Explain WHY You're Writing

Hi Bob, I just want/wanted to let you know that blah blah blah…

I am writing because I couldn't wait to tell you about blah blah blah…

I'm just writing to tell you about blah blah blah…

How to Say 'Sorry'

I want to apologize for…..

I want to say sorry for blah blah blah…

Sorry for blah blah blah…

How to Ask for Help

I was wondering if you'd help me (out) with blah blah blah…

I'd be really grateful if you could blah blah blah…

I was just wondering if you could do me a big favor.

Expressing Happiness

I was absolutely thrilled to hear that/about blah blah blah….

I'm over the moon to hear that/about blah blah blah….

How to Deliver Negative News

I'm afraid blah blah blah….

Unfortunately, blah blah blah….

Regrettably, blah blah blah….

I've got some bad news for you.

Ending an Email or Letter

Take care.

Hope to see you soon.

Looking forward to hearing from you.

Keep in touch.

Can't wait to see you soon.

I look forward to catching up.

All the best.

Don't be a stranger!

Organization & Focus

You still have to remember what you're doing and make it very clear in the letter. Are you thanking the person, are you answering a question, are you asking for something, are you offering advice? Make this clear right away in the introduction. Make sure the body follows.

Language

Again, you don't want to use very serious language in an informal letter or email; you don't want to use too many formal or complex words because that's not how we usually speak to friends and family.

With our friends, we're usually very casual and relaxed.

For example:

I just wanted to say thanks for helping me out last week.

In a formal letter, you would write

I'm writing to express my appreciation and gratitude for your assistance with last week's matter...

Notice the different feel of the two sentences. One is very casual; one is very formal.

Another example:

Should you require any further information, please do not hesitate to contact me - formal.

Versus

Let me know if you need anything else - super casual.

To make your letter look real, the best thing you can do is ALWAYS rely on your personal experience.

You **must** distinguish between formal and informal language in English, not only for this exam but also for general communication. Writing a letter or email to a friend is not the same as writing a letter of recommendation for a friend who has applied for a job. Here are some examples of formal and informal words with the same meaning,

VERBS:

FORMAL: INFORMAL

to depart: to go

to carry out: to do

to provide: to give

to retain: keep

to cease: stop

to seek: look for

assist, aid: to help

liberate: to free

obtain: to get

to desire: want

request: to ask for

to function: work

to demonstrate: show

to reside: live

require: need

OTHER WORDS:

FORMAL: INFORMAL

subsequently: next / later

immature, infantile: childish

sufficient: enough

further: more (information)

hence, therefore: so

deficiency, lack of: little, there is no

perspiration: sweat

inexpensive: cheap

☐

- IELTS ESSAYS: Task 2 IELTS Academic & General Training Exams-

Introduction

- Task 2 is exactly the same in both the Academic exam and the General exam.
- You will need to write an essay in response to an opinion, an argument, or a problem.
- Your essay must be written in formal English.

Types of IELTS Essay

1. Opinion Essay (Agree or Disagree)

2. Advantages & Disadvantages Essay

3. Problem & Solution Essay

4. Discussion Essay

5. Two-part Essay Question

How Many Words Should I Write in the IELTS Essay?

- In task 2, you should write at least 250 words

- You should spend 40 minutes on it

Two Common Problems in the Exam...

Problem 1- NOT ENOUGH Words:

- Less than 250 words MIGHT lower your score (you might not explain your ideas very well).

Problem 2- TOO MANY Words:

- You might be using too many words.

- You might be trying to express too much information.

This means:

- You might run out of time during the exam.

- The longer your essay is, the more probability you have of making grammar and vocabulary mistakes.

- If you write too many words in Task 2, you will have less time to complete task 1.

Sentence Structures

"The English language is an arsenal of weapons. If you are going to brandish them without checking to see whether or not they are loaded, you must expect to have them explode in your face from time to time." ~ *Stephen Fry*

- Every sentence has its own purpose.

- Treat each sentence like **gold**: there should be no useless sentences in your essay

- Plan your sentences: you need to make sure every piece of your essay fits together

- Be concise: don't fall into the trap of trying to make every sentence longer and more complicated just to fill space.

- Write your essay like a human being is going to read it!

Paragraph Structures

A paragraph normally has three parts:

1. One sentence to introduce the general topic we will write about in the paragraph (you also normally need to link the first sentence to the previous paragraph).

2. Two or three sentences that develop the topic in more detail. In the IELTS exam, you usually need to include evidence, examples, and details about the topic or argument.

3. A concluding sentence that either finishes the topic (or links it to the next paragraph).

Understanding the Topic and the Task

- Make sure you understand what the topic or subject of questions is. Underline the keywords if necessary.

- Read the questions carefully to identify exactly what you need to.

- Focus on the question itself, not on what you want to write about.

There usually are three ways the essay can be presented in the exam. Let's take the example of space exploration:

Type 1: Two **opposite views** to discuss:

"Some people believe that more funds should be invested in space exploration, as it is a vital form of investigation for the future of humanity. In contrast, others believe it is a waste of vital funding that could otherwise be used towards more essential projects here on earth. "

Type 2: "Two **opposite views** to discuss using the word *should* in the instruction.

"Should more money be invested into space exploration, or should it be used towards more important projects here on Earth?"

Type 3: A **statement** to discuss:

- "Paying for space exploration is a waste of vital funding which could otherwise be used towards more important projects here on earth."

The Beginning of the Essay

To get the highest grades in the IELTS exam, the essay has to introduce the topic, so you must begin with a relatively general statement. However, the trick is not to over-generalise; otherwise, the statement becomes meaningless.

For example, the following first sentence is meaningless, and the structure used is not appropriate.

There are those who argue that water is necessary for human life, and therefore, water shortage is one of the most important problems in the world.

Comments

Water is vital to human life, and this is an absolute fact, not something that people can argue about. The student wanted to use '*There are those who argue that,*' but this structure is wrong for the meaning of the sentence. The statement is also too general, and it is not clear what this essay is about.

Possible improvement

Water shortages affect millions of people worldwide each year, and there is evidence that suggests that they are becoming increasingly difficult to tackle due to climate change.

It is a bad idea to memorize words or structures ('*There are those who argue that,*' '*nobody would dispute the fact that...*' etc.) to insert your ideas into.

Each sentence and paragraph is like a house that needs logical, solid foundations before you decorate it.

It is better to start with your ideas and then think about how you can express them best.

Connecting Paragraphs to Each Other

When you start a new paragraph, you tell the reader that the previous point is finished and you are creating something new. Nevertheless, this new paragraph is not disconnected from the previous one, and you need to communicate to the reader what the connection is. For instance, if you start with *However, there are those who argue that violence is not something we learn from television and computer games...* then the structure you have used signals to the reader that you are discussing a different argument (*'However,'*) which contradicts the previous ideas, and *'there are those who argue that..',* which is expressed by other people, not you. You have communicated a lot of information to the reader with only seven words (*However, there are those who argue that…*). This is one of the definitions of good writing. Effective, while using as few words as possible to maintain clarity.

"Another argument is that...."

If you start a new paragraph with the phrase *'Another argument in favor of stricter laws is that crime is directly related to…' then you are signaling to the reader that you are changing to a different argument ('Another') with the same purpose ('in favor of..').*

To give more specific information, use *'This argument ...'.*

This is a handy structure to learn, and it can be adapted to many different contexts.

Here is an example of how we can use this structure in an essay.

There is no doubt that corruption is the most crucial point to focus on because it originates from positions of power. Corruption can take many shapes and forms, such as political, which involves crimes in a country's legal system and within the police, and economic, for example, by misusing tax money. All the evidence suggests that countries with corrupt governments are not able to develop as fast as countries where there is less corruption.

These factors [...].

OR

This negative environment [...].

The first sentence of a paragraph is vital, as it shows how it connects with the overall structure and can signal what will happen next.

When you practice writing, always check that your essay is logical by underlining the most important sentences in each paragraph. You should be able to understand the whole essay only by reading those sentences. If you can't, you need to make changes.

Expressing the Importance of the Topic

Superlatives can be useful to indicate that the topic is important:

		causes of ...	is ...
(one of) **the most**		problems of ...	
(some of) **the most**	significant important	conditions for ...	are ...
		aspects of ...	

			causes of ...
		significant	problems of ...
... is	(one of) **the most**	important	conditions for ...
			aspects of ...

Efficiency

Efficient writing expresses an idea, opinion, reason, or consequence without using too many words. Many students make a big mistake because they try to fill the page with words thinking this will make them finish the essay sooner and look good. After all, it means they know a lot. This is entirely wrong for most, if not all, exams, whether it's the IELTS or a university exam. Always use the minimum number of words possible, and do not repeat yourself.

According to Google, the definition of efficiency is: "*maximum productivity with minimum wasted effort or expense.*" In your writing, this means few words but lots of meaning.

Note: remember that in the IELTS, the word count indicated in the exam is a minimum, not a maximum, so you still need to reach this minimum, or you will be penalized, but you should avoid repetition and meaningless sentences by carefully proofreading your writing before you finish.

Using nouns in your essay

If you pay attention to the best essay examples and the best academic writing in general, you will notice that many noun phrases are used.

Here is an example:

"*At an investigative level, the availability of digital resources, simulators, and other tools provide the researcher with increased access to information.* "

A large portion of that sentence is made up of nouns. Using nouns is hugely efficient, whereas using verbs can be long and repetitive in an essay or description sometimes.

Ideally, you should combine both structures to add variety and power to your writing.

Exercise

Change the sentences by using nouns instead of verbs where possible.

The trick is to find the verbs first, then transform some of them into nouns, e.g.:

The area would benefit if businesses increased the amount they produced.

The area would benefit from an increase in business productivity/ business production.

1. The local government should train their employees better so that they can be more efficient.

   ....

   ....

2. There are differences between cultures, so they need to communicate by using different strategies.

   ....

   ....

3. If governments around the world implement this strategy, they may reduce pollution.

....

....

4. If they recycle waste, they may have a better chance of reducing poverty in the area.

....

....

Suggested Answers

1. *Better employee training would increase the local government's efficiency. / With better employee training, the local government's efficiency would increase.*

2. *Cultural differences need/require a wide range of/different communication strategies.*

3. *The implementation of this strategy by (world) governments may lead to reductions in pollution.*

4. *The recycling of waste may improve the chances of reducing poverty in the area / may lead to a reduction of poverty in the area / may lead to an improved chance of reducing poverty in the area.*

Showing Balance in your Essay

The IELTS writing exam prepares you for writing within an academic and professional setting where you need to be respectful of others' ideas.

Use cautious language.

In your essays, it would look awful if you said something like, *'These people are completely wrong'* or *'I think these researchers were wrong.'* Instead, you would need to express yourself more diplomatically, for example: *'However, it might be the case that ....'* or *'Recent research suggests that this is not the case.'*

You are supposed to analyze different sides and project a sense of impartiality while you say whether you agree or disagree.

Remember, you always need to remain modest about your opinion and show the reader that you understand that you may be wrong, just like anybody else.

For example:

"Students have a very low level of basic mathematical knowledge due to over-dependence on calculators."

This is the student's personal opinion, but she/he cannot write this without evidence. In the IELTS exam, you are not likely going to be able to cite real evidence to support your arguments, so you need to change your language: *"Over-dependence on calculators **may** have a negative effect on the basic mathematical knowledge of **some students**."*

This is also called 'hedging' language because 'to hedge against something' means to protect yourself from its negative consequences.

Students often make the mistake of using cautious language where it is not appropriate. They sometimes use *'would,' 'might,' 'likely to,'* etc., because they have learned that these verbs are common in academic writing.

For example:

"Annual financial reports **<u>might</u>** **include information from financial statements and other sources."**

You don´t need to know a lot about accounting or business to understand that the objective of financial reports is to provide financial information taken from financial statements and other sources. Therefore, the verb *'might'* can´t be used here.

Remember...

Link your sentences in formal writing.

Always use Linking Adverbs like *therefore, additionally, consequently, firstly, secondly, finally, moreover, however*

Use synonyms to replace basic-level vocabulary.

To (purpose)= *in order to, so as to*

Like = *such as, for example, for instance*

Get = *receive, acquire, obtain*

Help = *aid, assist, support*

Not only does X do Y, but it also does Z

Look at the difference between these sentences...

Version 1: *Working gives you the experience to help your career prospects. Working also improves essential skills like social skills.*

Version 2: *Not only does working provide you with experience to help your career prospects, but it also improves essential skills such as social interaction and communication.*

Focus on the Topic and the Task

Task 2 in the IELTS writing exam is essential if you want to get a high band score in the exam. It is easy to considerably improve your writing score as long as you are prepared to take some advice and practice, practice, practice.

Essay instructions have two parts. You must understand both the topic and the task before you start the essay.

The first part tells you the topic of the essay:

Some people believe that more funds should be invested into space exploration as it is a vital form of investigation for the future of humanity, while others believe it is a waste of vital funding that could otherwise be used towards more essential projects here on Earth.

OR

Space exploration is much too expensive, and the money should be spent on more important things.

OR

Despite the availability of numerous gyms, many people are living more sedentary lifestyles.

The second part of the question gives you the specific task you must complete to get marks:

Advantages & Disadvantages with your opinion: *Discuss both these views and give your own opinion.*

Or

Only your opinion essay: *What is your opinion?*

Or

Problem essay: *What problems are associated with this?*

What solutions can you suggest?

Common Mistakes in the IELTS Essay

Don't use (...) or (etc.) when you are writing lists.

It looks lazy in an essay.

- Write lists like this; (A and B), (A, B, and C), or (A, B, C, and D).

- Example: "Some of the biggest issues humanity faces at the moment are pollution, poverty, disease, and global warming."

Don't use question marks in your essay:

- Don't ask the reader any questions in your essays.

  For example;

- "What is the best way to reduce pollution in developing countries?"-

Don't use exclamation marks!!!!!!!!!!

For example, "It is probably true to say that, on the whole, we use too much plastic!"

Use Formal English

- Use "an increasing number of" (countable) or "an increasing amount of" (uncountable) to mean "more."

- Instead of writing "more businesses are paying attention to climate and sustainability issues," you could use "an increasing number of."

- For example: "an increasing number of businesses are paying attention to climate and sustainability issues." instead of "more businesses…."

- Add "significantly more" to express "a lot more" or "significant" to mean "quite a lot."

- Example: "significantly more businesses are paying attention to climate and sustainability issues." instead of "quite a lot more businesses …"

- "a significant number of businesses are paying attention to climate and sustainability issues." OR "a sizeable number of businesses are paying attention to climate and sustainability issues." instead of "quite a lot of businesses…, or "a lot of businesses…."

- Use "a growing number of" (countable) or "growing amount of" (uncountable) to mean "more and more."

- Example: "A growing number of businesses are paying attention to climate and sustainability issues."

Avoid Contractions

- Avoid contractions in your essay!

  Examples:

- wouldn't = would not

- couldn't = could not

- mightn't = might not

- Etc.

"But," "And" & "Because"

- Avoid starting a sentence with "But" or "And."

- Use "Furthermore,...", "In addition,..." instead of "And."

- Use "However,..." instead of "But."

- Use "Since...", "As a result,..." instead of "Because..."

- There are instances when we can start a formal or semi-formal sentence with "Because," but the options above are better.

"Most" & "Almost"

- "Most" = adjective meaning the largest quantity, amount, degree, or number of….

- Followed by a noun, prepositional phrase, or adjective

- "Most proponents of…."

- "the most beneficial solution…."

- "In most cases…."

- "most of my peers…."

- "Almost" = adverb meaning nearly, not completely.

- "There are almost 700 million people living in extreme poverty, according to the World Bank."

- "Almost 10% of the world's population lives in extreme poverty, according to the World Bank."

Silly Mistakes

- Articles (a, an, no article)

- Subject-Verb Agreement

- Singular-Plural

- Countable/Uncountable Nouns

  * Learn how to use them in English and pay close attention when you are writing.

Avoid Personal Opinions in Body Paragraphs

- **Only for Introduction or conclusion (usually):**

  "I think"

  "I believe"

  "in my opinion."

- This is a general rule and does not mean you will automatically lose marks if you break it.

- However, you should definitely follow it to keep your essay well-structured.

- Use impersonal opinions in the body paragraphs

  "Some people believe that.... "

  "Others argue that.... "

  "There are those who claim that...."

  "It is probably true to say that.... "

  "Nobody would dispute the fact that..."

A Global Perspective

- Essay questions are asked from a global perspective

- Avoid relating the essay question only to your country unless the question tells you to do so.

- Use your personal experiences, but present them with a global perspective. You can do this by generalizing ideas, reactions, opinions, and experiences with language like *'Many people...', 'A large number of people/users/customers/holiday/makers, etc.'*

For example, instead of "Factories in my city release toxic waste into the river, but the government does nothing to stop them,"...

Write: *"Factories across the world release toxic waste into water supplies, but many governments are unable to stop them.."*

Use linking words

- Start body paragraphs and conclusion with linking words and transition phrases.

- Keep your sentences short and well-linked.

- You will get marks for organization if you do this right.

For example

- Firstly,... Secondly,... Thirdly,...

- On the one hand,.... On the other hand,...

- To sum up, ...

Personal Pronouns

Avoid using personal pronouns in the body paragraphs of your essay if possible.

You should delete or rephrase:

Me, you, I, we, us,

You can rephrase it as:

Workers, inhabitants, businesses, young people, students, people, society, etc.

For example:

Instead of: "If I study at university, I will have more career opportunities."

Write: "If people/young people/students study at university, they will have more career opportunities."

Be Realistic in Your Language

- Unless you are presenting a 100% fact like *"Water begins to boil at 100°C"* ...

- Make sure your sentences show that you understand that what you say is not always true in every case!

- Avoid using words like;

- *all / every / none / only / always / never / totally / completely*

- Be careful with this language!

- For example: "When people start a new job, they feel anxious...."

- Should be: "Many people feel anxious when they start a new job...."

- "All students need help with accommodation when they start at university."

- Should be: "A large number of (Many) students need help with accommodation when they start at university."

Avoid Using "Thing"

For example

- Instead of "When students get their first job, they are able to learn many new <u>things</u>."

- Write, "When students get their first job, they are able to learn many new <u>skills</u>, such as time- management, interpersonal communication, and goal-setting."

- You are avoiding the word "thing," which is vague, and you are giving specific examples.

Chapter 11. Opinion Essays

Two Types of Opinion Essay Questions:

There are two main types of Opinion Essay in the IELTS test:

Type 1: Opinion essays where the exam question gives you both sides of an argument.

Type 2: Opinion essays where only one side is presented in the question.

Type 1: Both sides given in the question

Typical end question(s):

- "What is your opinion?"

Full Question Example:

Some people believe that violence on TV, in films, and in computer games has a damaging effect on society. Others deny that these factors have any significant influence on people's behavior. What is your opinion?

Tactics:

You can…

- Agree 100% with one side

- Partly Agree with one side

Type 2: One side given in the question

Typical end question(s):

- "Do you agree?"

- or "What is your opinion?"

- or "To what extent do you agree?"

Full Question Example:

Some people believe that violence on TV, in films, and in computer games has a damaging effect on society. What is your opinion?

Tactics:

You can…

- Agree 100%

- Disagree 100%

- Partly Agree

How to Agree 100% with One Side

In the example below, we will look at a Type 2 question that only gives one side of the argument. However, you can use the following approach for both types of questions, so don't worry.

Example Question:

According to some people, students from all economic backgrounds should be able to attend university. They believe that the government should provide free university education for everyone.

Do you agree with this view?

In other words…. The above question is asking you:

Do you agree that the government should provide free university for everyone?

- You need to decide whether you think that university education should be paid for by the students (disagree), …or whether you think it should be paid for by the government (agree).

- Then, give reasons why.

- In our example response, we are going to say, "agree."

Planning & Brainstorming Process:

1. It's crucial to have your paragraph ideas and supporting reasons planned in note form **before** you start writing.

- Students who don't do this often get confused and have to rewrite sections of their essays.

- They lose marks for having a disorganized, unclear essay

- Or they lose marks for running out of time and not finishing their essay

2. When you have your ideas and your supporting reasons for each idea, your essay will be MUCH easier to write!

- You will feel less stressed and have a more clear focus.

- Therefore, you will likely get better grades in the exam.

Note-taking During Planning:

The following is a simulation of the notes you could make while you are planning your essay.

Notes:

Question: *Do you agree that the government should provide free university for everyone?*

Answer: *Yes.*

Because....

Reasons:

Reason 1: *Without financial support, many students who want to go to university have no other way to fulfill their dreams, + those who work and study will have worse results.*

Reason 2: *Educating the population is a long-term investment into the future of any country. No country can prosper without an educated population.*

Detailed notes for Reasons 1 and 2:

1. *Without financial support, many students who want to go to university have no other way to fulfill their dreams, + those who work and study will have worse results.*

- *Many learners are unable to pay for their university education, even though they really want degrees.*

- *Even when students can afford to pay for university, they often have to take out loans and work part-time to pay for their living costs.*

- *This can severely affect grades and future career development.*

- *It can also leave them with large debts to pay when they finish studying.*

2. *Educating the population is a long-term investment in the future of any country. No country can prosper without an educated population.*

- *For example, taxpayers' money is misused by the government on initiatives like space exploration.*

- *If a country can't educate its population, there is no sense in investing large amounts of money into ambitious space projects.*

- *A more sensible distribution of government funds could allow many students to fulfill their dreams.*

- *A more educated society, which would benefit the country as a whole for many years (to come).*

IELTS Essay Planning Tips Summary (One-sided Opinion Essay)

1. Find the main opinion expressed in the essay question.

2. Decide if you agree or disagree.

3. Brainstorm main points

4. Short notes about supporting reasons

Introduction

In the following section, we are going to look at how you can write the introduction part of your IELTS essay. If you follow these steps and practice regularly before the exam, you will find great success.

Exam Question:

According to some people, students from all economic backgrounds should be able to attend university. They believe that the government should provide free university education for everyone.

Do you agree with this view?

1st - Paraphrase the Issue

The first thing you need to do is paraphrase the issue that the question is focusing on. Use synonyms, turns of phrase, and colocations to do this. Here is a good example of how you can change the sentence without losing its meaning and show the examiner that you have an excellent command of English:

Original sentence(s):

According to some people, students from all economic backgrounds should be able to attend university. They believe that the government should provide free university education for everyone.

Paraphrased Version:

The question of whether or not_the government should consider making tertiary education freely available to all learners has been the subject of recent/ heated public discussion/ debate.

What exactly have we changed?

"university education"

"tertiary education." These are essentially the same thing.

"provide free university education."

Has become "make tertiary education freely available."

"Students from all economic backgrounds"

has become "all learners."

We've also added the standard sentence structure: *The question of whether or not .... has been the subject of recent/heated public discussion.*

This structure is very useful so that we can comfortably paraphrase the issue.

2nd - Answer the Question

Original Question:

Do you agree with this view?

Answer:

Higher education, in my opinion, should be free regardless of income, based on the grounds that it would benefit both individuals and society.

What synonyms have we used?

In this part of our introduction, we've used another synonym for "university education," "higher education." Then, to add extra variety to our language, we've used "on the grounds that" instead of "because." We've then moved on to specifying *why* we think higher education should be free without being too specific (*it would benefit both individuals and society*).

So there you have it, that's all you need to do to write your introduction for the IELTS essay. Here is the full version of the paragraph we've just written together.

The question of whether or not the government should consider making tertiary education freely available to all learners has been the subject of recent/ heated public discussion/ debate. Higher education, in my opinion, should be free regardless of income, based on the grounds that it would benefit both individuals and society.

Body Paragraph 1

In this paragraph, we are going to fully explain the first reason why we believe that university should be free for all learners.

Structure:

1- State One Reason or Argument

2- Expand/Explain

3- Example

This 1st sentence connects to the question and gives a reason why you agree.

Firstly, one argument in favor of eliminating university fees is that there are many learners who are unable to pay for their education, despite their strong desire to obtain degrees.

What vocabulary have we used so far?

Firstly,

This indicates to the examiner that we are listing our first argument.

one argument in favor of…

This connects our new paragraph back to the question and tells the examiner that we are going to give an argument in favor of free university education.

eliminating university fees

We are paraphrasing the issue with the verb "eliminating", as another way of saying that the government should provide free education for all students.

unable to pay

We are using "unable to pay", as a formal substitute for "can't pay." This shows the examiner that the writer knows and can use different options depending on the context they are writing in.

their education

We are using a more general synonym here to write about university education. Even though "education" is more general than "university education," "tertiary education," and "higher education," we don't need to specify this time, as we have already mentioned it clearly in the essay. Using some slightly more general terms once you've specified is a great way of adding variety to your writing and showing the examiner your command of English.

The rest of the paragraph explains why this is important. We will then give an example, adopting a 'world view,' before giving details of the negative consequences of not helping students.

Why this is important:

Without sufficient financial support/backing, these students have no other way to fulfill their dreams.

Give an example, adopting a 'world view':

Even in cases where students can afford to pay for university, they often have to take out loans and work part-time to pay for their living costs.

Give details of the negative consequences of not helping students:

This can severely affect their grades and, therefore, their future career development. It can also leave them with large debts to pay when they finish studying. These financial barriers may discourage highly talented students from pursuing a university education.

So, the entire first body paragraph would look like this:

Firstly, one argument in favor of eliminating university fees is that there are many learners who are unable to pay for their education despite their strong desire to obtain degrees. Without sufficient financial support, these students have no other way to fulfill their dreams. Even in cases where students can afford to pay for university, they often have to take out loans and work part-time to pay for their living costs. This can severely affect their grades and, therefore, their future career development. It can also leave them with large debts to pay when they finish studying. These financial barriers may discourage highly talented students from pursuing a university education.

Body Paragraph 2

Again, in this paragraph, we are going to fully explain the second reason why we believe that university should be free for all learners.

Structure:

1- State One Reason or Argument

2- Expand/Explain

3- Example

This 1ˢᵗ sentence connects to the question and gives a reason why you agree.

Secondly, no country can prosper without an educated population, so funding free university education is a long-term investment into the future of the country.

Give an example, adopting a 'world view' or a 'society-wide view':

Taxpayers' money is arguably being misused by governments on initiatives like space exploration.

Give details of the negative consequences of not helping students AND the benefits of helping them:

If a country can't educate its population, there is no sense in investing large amounts of money into ambitious space projects. A far more sensible distribution of government funds could allow thousands of students to fulfill their dreams. This would lead to a more educated society, which would, no doubt, benefit the country as a whole for many years (to come).

So, the entire second body paragraph would look like this:

Secondly, no country can prosper without an educated population, so funding free university education is a long-term investment into the future of the country. Taxpayers' money is arguably being misused by the government on initiatives like space exploration. If a country can't educate its population, there is no sense in investing large amounts of money into ambitious space projects. A far more sensible distribution of government funds could allow thousands of students to fulfill their dreams. This would lead to a more educated society, which would, no doubt, benefit the country as a whole for many years (to come).

Conclusion

In the conclusion part of your essay, you should give a summary of the main points you've mentioned and then restate your opinion so that you finish with a clear message.

Conclusion

1- Summary of Main Points

2- Restate opinion

Summary of main points:

In conclusion, free university education, regardless of income, is crucial for any society seeking sustainable progress. Expensive tuition fees may discourage some individuals from pursuing university degrees, as young people are often unwilling to carry the burden of their loans for many years after graduation, making university less appealing.

Restate opinion:

The government should be responsible for the cost of tertiary education. Hence, it would be appropriate for the government to distribute financial resources better in order to do this.

So the conclusion paragraph would be:

In conclusion, free university education, regardless of income, is crucial for any society seeking sustainable progress. Expensive tuition fees may discourage some individuals from pursuing university degrees, as young people are often unwilling to carry the burden of their loans for many years after graduation, making university less appealing. The government should be responsible for the cost of tertiary education. Hence, it would be appropriate for the government to distribute financial resources better in order to do this.

Linking Words

1. Use linking words like *firstly, secondly, thirdly, etc.* They are relatively simple and make it easier for the examiner to follow the development of your ideas.

You can use them to separate paragraphs like in the example above, or you can use them to separate reasons (evidence) within the same paragraphs like we've done in the example below:

Several studies have proven that global warming is already having a negative impact on human life. <u>Firstly</u>, it has been shown to affect crops worldwide, leading to significant shortages in some cases. <u>Secondly</u>, global temperature increases have compromised food production in some regions, which has caused inflation and a deterioration of the quality of life of the people affected. <u>Thirdly</u>, it causes unnecessary stress and, in some cases, conflict within already vulnerable sectors of the world population.

Repetition

Repetition can be good sometimes if you do it for a good reason.

- Using repetition, you improve comprehension.

- You can use synonyms to repeat important parts of your ideas.

- The examiner can't read your mind, so repeating yourself sometimes reminds the examiner about what you are talking about!

Check out the example below to see how you can use repetition to create a strong paragraph.

Several studies have proven that <u>global warming</u> is already having a negative impact on human life. Firstly, it has been shown to affect crops worldwide, leading to significant shortages in some cases. Secondly, <u>global temperature increases</u> have compromised food production in some regions, <u>which</u> has caused inflation and a deterioration of the quality of life of the people affected. Thirdly, <u>rising temperatures</u> are causing unnecessary stress, and in some cases conflict, within already vulnerable sectors of the world population.

Special Vocabulary

- *Tertiary education, higher education, university education*

- *Income- money you receive*

- *Sufficient - enough*

- *Financial support - funding*

- *Government funds - Government funding -Government money - Government resources*

- *Fulfill – reach (ambitions, dreams, etc.)*

- *, no doubt - undoubtedly*

- *Years to come- years in the future*

- *Sustainable progress- healthy growth*

- *Discourage X from –ing - stop X from -ing*

- *(are) unwilling to- don't want to*

- *Carry the burden of – take on the responsibility of*

- *Less appealing - Less attractive*

- *Hence, - Therefore,*

Balanced Opinion Essay (Taking Ideas from Both Sides)

- This style of essay takes ideas from both sides of the issue.

- Doesn't completely agree with both sides but agrees with SOME aspects of both arguments.

- Doesn't discuss both sides robotically but instead expresses a CLEAR opinion based on logic.

Balanced Opinion Essay Example

Certain people truly believe that planning for the future is a complete waste of time. They think that the present should be the main focus.

Do you agree with this view?

Introduction

1. Paraphrase:

Some people think that living for the moment and enjoying the present is more important than making plans for the future.

2. Give Clear Opinion

In my opinion, a life without any planning for the future can be chaotic and stressful. So, while it is important to be present and enjoy the moment, a degree of planning is always required in order to live a full, happy life.

So, the introduction would look like this:

Some people think that living for the moment and enjoying the present is more important than making plans for the future. In my opinion, a life without any planning for the future can be chaotic and stressful. So, while it is important to be present and enjoy the moment, a degree of planning is always required in order to live a full, happy life.

Body Paragraphs

- ALWAYS plan your body paragraphs

- DO NOT get distracted and go deep into discussing advantages and disadvantages

Quick Plan:

Body Paragraph 1: Stress and physical health

Body Paragraph 2: Motivation + life or career goals

Body Paragraph 3: Planning is compatible with focusing on the present. It's about balance.

Body Paragraph 1 Plan

- People who have goals generally understand what they want in life and have more confidence in their decisions.

- Because of this, they are happier and more successful in many cases.

- Never knowing what you need to do next or constantly making mistakes and forgetting important things can be very stressful and affect your quality of life. It can also affect your long-term health.

Body Paragraph 1 Example

It is probably true to say that people who have goals generally understand what they want in life and, as a result, have more confidence in their decisions since they have usually thought them through and planned them. This leads to higher levels of long-term happiness and success in many cases. Never knowing what you need to do next or constantly making mistakes and forgetting important events can be highly stressful and severely affect your quality of life, as well as your long-term health.

Body Paragraph 2 Example

Furthermore, making plans for the future provides people with motivation. In fact, most individuals are motivated by a vision they have for their future. Making plans for the future renders a person's growth more feasible. It is true that even the most successful people can become distracted and discouraged at times. As a result, they may find it difficult to fully appreciate their accomplishments and enjoy their success. Having clearly defined goals can help minimize this issue.

Body Paragraph 3 Example

Finally, a balanced lifestyle that includes specific and realistic goals, together with a healthy amount of focus on the present, is more likely to lead to long-term happiness and fulfillment. There is evidence that suggests that purposefully focusing on the present can be part of a healthy, balanced lifestyle. Practices such as mindfulness and meditation, for instance, have numerous reported benefits, such as reducing stress and even blood pressure.

Conclusion

In conclusion, I believe that developing a long-term strategy and concentrating on the present are not mutually exclusive. Concentrating on clear goals helps individuals to become more organized in their daily lives and happier overall. As a result, it would be better if people started planning for their futures as soon as possible, but without neglecting their short-term happiness and well-being.

Balanced Opinion Essay Recap

- Clearly written opinion in the Introduction section

- Does not contradict itself.

- Body paragraphs explain the opinion in more detail and give clear reasons for the opinion

Chapter 12. Advantages & Disadvantages Essay

Types of Question

There are two main types of 'IELTS advantages and disadvantages' essay questions:

Type 1: Questions that ask for your opinion.

Type 2: Questions that do not require you to state your opinion.

Typical Question Words

Advantages & Disadvantages Essay with Opinion

"Do the benefits outweigh the drawbacks?"

"Do the advantages outweigh the disadvantages?"

"What are the advantages and disadvantages of....?"

"Discuss the advantages and disadvantages. Give your opinion."

Example:

A lot of countries rely on tourism as a main source of income. However, tourism can also cause problems if it is not managed correctly.

Describe the advantages and disadvantages of international tourism in today's modern world. Do you believe that the benefits of tourism outweigh its drawbacks?

You should:

Write about **advantages** and **disadvantages** and say if it's mostly positive or negative based on your analysis.

Advantages & Disadvantages Essay WITHOUT Opinion

"Discuss the advantages and disadvantages."

"Discuss the advantages and disadvantages."

Example:

A lot of countries rely on tourism as a main source of income. However, tourism can also cause problems if it is not managed correctly.

Discuss the advantages and disadvantages of tourism in the modern world.

You should:

Write about **+** and **−**

Full Task Example

When individuals with cultural differences work and live together, they are said to be living in a multi-cultural society.

Do you believe that the advantages of living in a multicultural society outweigh the disadvantages?

How to Brainstorm Ideas

Advantages of Multi-Cultural Society

- Allows people to broaden their understanding of the world - more tolerance and improved relations among communities.

- Can give a place a unique mix, which adds to its identity.

- Can boost the local economy, providing jobs and prosperity.

Disadvantages of Multi-Cultural Society

- Can lead to conflict and resentment if not managed properly.

Notes on Tactics

We need to pick a side and be tactical in our response to this question. We might not be able to explain the disadvantage we came up with properly in such a short essay since the issue is very complex. Therefore, we are going to say that the advantages outweigh the disadvantages, and we are going to treat this disadvantage superficially to save space and time. It's too complex to explain fully in a short paragraph.

General Structure

Introduction

1- Paraphrase Question

2- State Opinion

Main Body Paragraph 1

1- State One Advantage

2- Expand/Explain

3- Example

Main Body Paragraph 2

1- State One Advantage

2- Expand/Explain

3- Example

Main Body Paragraph 3

1- State One Disadvantage

2- Expand/Explain

3- Example

Conclusion

1- Summary of Main Points

2- Restate opinion

Introduction

Essay Question:

When individuals with cultural differences work and live together, they are said to be living in a multi-cultural society.

Do you believe that the advantages of living in a multicultural society outweigh the disadvantages?

Exercise

1st - Identify and paraphrase the issue that the question is asking you to write about.

What is the issue?

The issue is whether, overall, multicultural societies are better or worse for the people who live in them.

Then, paraphrase the Issue in the question and check your answer below.

....

Answer

The question of whether the benefits of living in a multicultural society outweigh its drawbacks has been sparking debate for several years.

2nd - Answer the Question

Write your answer to the essay question. Then, compare your answer to the example. Remember, you don't have to agree with our example; it is only there to guide you in terms of language and style.

. . . .

Answer

I believe that having individuals with different cultural backgrounds work and live together is beneficial on many levels and that, therefore, the advantages clearly outweigh the disadvantages.

Therefore, this is what the introduction paragraph looks like…

The question of whether the benefits of living in a multicultural society outweigh the drawbacks has been sparking debate for several years. I believe that having individuals with different cultural backgrounds work and live together is beneficial on many levels and that, therefore, the advantages clearly outweigh the disadvantages.

Body Paragraph 1

1- State One Advantages

2- Expand/Explain

3- Example

Exercise

As we saw in the Opinion Essay, the first sentence connects to the topic of the question and signals to the reader what we are going to discuss. The first sentence, in this case, connects to the question and signals to the reader that we are going to talk about advantages.

The formula we are going to use here is X creates a variety of advantages. So, what is X in this case? Look at the essay question again and solve it.

Essay Question:

When individuals with cultural differences work and live together, they are said to be living in a multi-cultural society.

Do you believe that the advantages of living in a multicultural society outweigh the disadvantages?

Answer

X, in this case, is *"Living and working in a diverse society,"* or *"multi-cultural living,"* or any other variation of this.

So, our first sentence in this paragraph is something like this:

Living and working in a diverse society creates a variety of advantages.

The rest of the paragraph explains the advantage(s)…

Write the rest of this paragraph and then check the example on the next page.

....

Example Answer:

For starters, multicultural environments allow people to broaden their understanding of the world and of human nature. Different cultures produce different perspectives and ideas, which help people learn more about the world. Having people from different parts of the world living together in the same region can provide excellent learning opportunities, as people are exposed to a variety of languages, cultures, and traditions. People can experience different foods and customs every day, leading to more tolerance and improved relations among communities.

Body Paragraph 2

1- State One Advantage

2- Expand/Explain

3- Example

Exercise

We are going to signal to the reader that we will state another advantage in this paragraph:

Write the first sentence signaling to the reader that you will state another advantage in this paragraph. Start with *"Furthermore."* Compare your answer to the example on the next page. Remember, these exercises teach you to write responses properly so that you can then state your opinion freely. The opinions expressed in the examples are not what's important for the purpose of this book.

. . . .

Example Answer

Furthermore, individuals from a variety of cultural backgrounds benefit society in many other ways.

We will now use an example to expand and explain this advantage. Write your answer below and then compare it to the example at the bottom of this page.

....

Answer

Because of their multicultural nature, countries like Australia, the UK, and Canada run a variety of yearly events to celebrate the coming together of different cultures.

The formula for this is as follows: *"Because of their multi-cultural nature, countries like X, Y, and Z run a variety of yearly events to celebrate the coming together of different cultures."*

X, Y, and Z, can be virtually any countries you want.

We now expand on and explain the advantage(s). Write your answer below and then compare it to the example on the next page.

....

Example Answer

These festivals serve as tourist attractions that boost the local economy, providing jobs and prosperity. These celebrations have the added effect of solidifying the area's identity and uniting people in celebration, which arguably contributes to a healthier, happier society.

As you can see, it doesn't matter which order you choose with the example and explanation. You can use your example to expand and explain, or you can expand and explain and then include an example to support your claims.

Body Paragraph 3

First, we are going to signal to the reader that we will be talking about a disadvantage here. So, language like *"one potential stumbling block is…"* is very useful. As soon as we've done this, we will state exactly what that disadvantage is so we're not wasting too many words.

Exercise

Write your own version of this sentence, then check the example on the next page.

Start your sentence with *"One potential stumbling block is …."* or *"One potential disadvantage is …."* or *"One potential issue is …."* or *"One potential problem is …."*

....

Example

One potential stumbling block is if the situation is not managed correctly and new communities do not become integrated.

Now that we've stated our disadvantage, we will expand and explain a bit. Write the rest of this paragraph and then check your answer by comparing it to our example. Please remember that your opinions may differ from the ones expressed in our example.

. . . .

Example Answer

This can lead to a feeling of isolation which often causes conflict and resentment if not managed properly.

We will now give what could be considered as an example, even though we are keeping it very general in this case. We will finish the example by explaining the disadvantage in a little more detail and by being more specific.

Furthermore, if communities become entrenched in specific areas within a city, and there are insufficient resources to serve all communities equally, this can result in further conflict, as a feeling of injustice becomes widespread.

The full body paragraph would be:

One potential stumbling block is if the situation is not managed correctly and new communities do not become integrated. This can lead to a feeling of isolation, which often causes conflict and resentment if not managed properly. Furthermore, if communities become entrenched in specific areas within a city, and there are insufficient resources to serve all communities equally, this can result in further conflict as a feeling of injustice becomes widespread.

Conclusion

1. Restate the Topic

Begin your conclusion by briefly restating the topic to remind the reader of what you've been discussing. Try to paraphrase your original thesis statement using different words to keep it fresh and engaging.

2. Summarize Key Points

Quickly summarize the main advantages and disadvantages you discussed in your body paragraphs. Focus on highlighting the most significant points that effectively convey your overall argument. This isn't about listing all the details again but emphasizing what you find most crucial.

3. Present a Balanced View

After your summary, present a balanced evaluation that reflects your understanding of the topic. Weigh the pros and cons you discussed and express which side you believe has more weight. This part of your conclusion should show your ability to critically assess and integrate the points discussed.

4. State or Imply a Conclusion

Clearly state whether you think the advantages outweigh the disadvantages or vice versa. If the topic is nuanced or if the scales don't tip clearly one way, it's fine to acknowledge this. You could suggest that the outcome depends on specific factors or personal perspectives.

5. Optional: Call to Action or Prediction

If it fits the prompt, you might conclude with a call to action or a prediction about the future. This can be particularly effective if the essay topic involves ongoing issues or developments that are expected to evolve.

Example Conclusion:

In conclusion, while the benefits of [topic], such as [brief summary of main advantages], are compelling, the drawbacks, including [brief summary of main disadvantages], present considerable challenges. Despite the merits of both sides, the advantages of [topic] seem to outweigh the disadvantages in certain contexts. Ultimately, the balance between these might vary based on individual situations and specific considerations.

Exercise

Essay Question:

When individuals with cultural differences work and live together, they are said to be living in a multi-cultural society.

Do you believe that the advantages of living in a multicultural society outweigh the disadvantages?

Write your conclusion to the example question.

Then, check the example on the next page.

- First, you should summarize the main points.

- Next, you should restate opinions.

....

Example Answer

First, we are going to summarize the main points.

After taking into consideration all of the points made above, I do not see any significant disadvantages to living in a multi-cultural environment, provided the situation is managed correctly, and all communities are fully integrated.

Next, we restate opinions.

I am confident that, in theory, the advantages clearly outweigh the disadvantages from both an economic and a cultural standpoint. Furthermore, I believe that in order to develop as a society and prosper in the long term, we must foster an atmosphere of respect and tolerance among cultures. Cultural diversity can enrich society on many levels and force us to confront our prejudices.

So, the full conclusion would be

After taking into consideration all of the points made above, I do not see any significant disadvantages to living in a multicultural environment, provided the situation is managed correctly and all communities are fully integrated. I am confident that, in theory, the advantages clearly outweigh the disadvantages from both an economic and a cultural standpoint. Furthermore, I believe that in order to develop as a society and prosper in the long term, we must foster an atmosphere of respect and tolerance among cultures. Cultural diversity can enrich society on many levels and force us to confront our prejudices.

Your Essay Checklist:

✓ Short and Sweet- To the point

✓ Effective paraphrase of the question in the Introduction

✓ Clear opinion in Introduction

✓ Consistent opinion throughout the whole essay

✓ Each body paragraph explains advantage or disadvantage + gives well-explained, logical examples where necessary.

✓ Conclusion summarizes opinion

Linking Words

- Use linking words like *"Furthermore,"* etc. These are quite straightforward and make it easier for the examiner to follow the development of your ideas.

- You can use them to separate paragraphs like in the example above, or you can use them to separate reasons (evidence) within the same paragraphs.

- Use synonyms to avoid excessive repetition:

Furthermore, individuals from a variety of cultural backgrounds benefit society in many other ways. Because of their multicultural nature, countries like Australia, the UK, and Canada run a variety of festivals to celebrate the coming together of different cultures. These festivals **serve as** *tourist attractions that boost the local economy, providing jobs and prosperity. These celebrations have the added effect of solidifying the area's identity and uniting people in celebration, which arguably contributes to a healthier, happier society.*

Special Vocabulary

Celebrations= Festivals= Street parties= Yearly events (these are not perfect synonyms, but can be used as synonyms when we are discussing festivals and celebrations in general)

Diverse= varied

Because of their multicultural nature,

Boost= enrich= improve

Solidify= consolidate= reinforce

Potential stumbling block= potential issue= possible problem

There are insufficient= there are not enough= there is a shortage of

(feeling of injustice) becomes widespread= feelings of injustice grows

from both an economic and a cultural standpoint= economically and culturally

we must foster= we must encourage

Cultural diversity can enrich society on many levels= Multiculturalism can improve society in many ways

Chapter 13. Problem & Solution Essay

There are three types of Problem-Solution Essay

- Problem and solution

- Cause and solution

- Just the solution

We will cover the most common type, which is problem-solution.

Cause- solution is exactly the same, but instead of analyzing the "problem," you analyze the "cause(s)" and then possible solutions.

It is very rare to get an essay where you only discuss solutions, but it is the easiest type: you focus 100% on solutions to the problem expressed in the question. The strategy is the same as what we will look at here.

Typical Question Phrases

To identify what type of Problem & Solution Essay question it is, you need to look out for specific language in the question.

Here are some typical phrases used in the exam.

Asking about the cause(s) or the problem(s):

➢ "What are some resulting issues, and how can they be addressed?"

➢ "What problems can this cause, and how can they be addressed?"

➢ "What issues arise from this, and how can we solve them?"

➢ "Why is this? How can it be solved?"

➢ "What is the reason for this, and what measures can be taken to solve the issue?"

Asking about the solution(s):

➢ "How can the problem be improved?"

➢ "What measures could be introduced to solve this?"

➢ "What solutions can be implemented to deal with the issue?"

➢ "How can this issue be resolved/prevented?"

Full Task Example

The number of people moving from rural to urban areas in search of a better life is increasing, but city life comes with its own set of issues.

What exactly are these issues, and how can they be solved?

Exercise:

Analyze the question and identify whether this essay question is a:

- Problem and solution

- Cause and solution

- Just the solution

Answer:

In this example, two questions have been phrased as one.

What are the <u>issues,</u> and how can they be <u>solved</u>?

Issues and solutions = therefore, it's a problem-solution essay.

2 Structures for Problem-Solution Essays

Both these structures would be the same length. It's up to you to choose the one you are most comfortable with.

Typical Structure 1 for Problem-Solution Essay

1. Introduction

2. Body paragraph 1: Identify and explain 2-3 issues

3. Body Paragraph 2: Explain the possible solutions

4. Conclusion

Typical Structure 2 for Problem-Solution Essay

1. Introduction

2. Body paragraph 1: Problem 1 + Solution

3. Body paragraph 2: Problem 2 + Solution

4. Body paragraph 3: Problem 3 + Solution

5. Conclusion

Common Mistakes

- Using too many ideas.

- Not writing enough detail about each idea.

- Not linking problems and solutions.

- Not being specific enough in explanations and examples or not taking a world view on the issue.

How To Understand Problem-Solution Essay Questions

The first thing you need to do is analyze the question

This is a crucial part of the planning process and will help you answer the question properly. This is crucial if you want to get an advanced grade (Bands 7-9).

1. General Topic words

Topic words describe the general subject of the question.
*The number **of people moving from rural to urban areas** in search of a better life is increasing, but city life comes with its own set of **issues**.*

So, the question is about 'issues or problems' connected to 'city life.'

Many IELTS candidates write about causes here, but you don't have any time or space for this!

2. Instruction words

Instruction words tell you what specific ideas the examiner wants you to write about:

What** exactly **are** these **issues, and** how can they **be solved?

This question tells us that the examiner wants to read about issues (problems) and solutions.

Brainstorming Ideas

You need to come up with some ideas to write about.

Write ideas as they come to your mind without worrying about high-level language or sounding amazing in English!

Just write ideas as if you were having an informal chat with a family member or a friend.

If you do it this way, you will come up with more ideas, as your brain won't be distracted by thinking about high-level vocabulary.

Here are some ideas for the example essay question we looked at:

Problems	Solutions
• Lots of people in the same space- Not enough housing	• Provide more affordable housing in city centers
• Traffic	• Better public transport
• Pollution + all its health risks	• Awareness campaigns + car-free zones like in London, Madrid, or Paris.

Introduction

Essay Question:

The number of people moving from rural to urban areas in search of a better life is increasing, but city life comes with its own set of issues.

What exactly are these issues, and how can they be solved?

Exercise

1st - Paraphrase the Issue:

Write a sentence to paraphrase the issue.

....

Example Answer:

A growing number of people are relocating from rural to urban areas in search of a better quality of life.

2nd – Give Some Details

Write 1-2 sentences giving some details.

....

Example Answer

However, problems such as <u>housing shortages, traffic congestion, and pollution</u> *can have a serious impact on that quality of life. This essay will examine these issues and propose potential solutions.*

So the whole introduction looks like this:

A growing number of people are relocating from rural to urban areas in search of a better quality of life. However, problems such as housing shortages, traffic congestion, and pollution can have a serious impact on that quality of life. This essay will examine these issues and propose potential solutions.

Body Paragraph 1

The first issue + solution…

This 1st sentence connects to the question and signals what we are going to talk about.

Write here, then check the example answer below. Start with *"Firstly,…"*

....

Example Answer

Firstly, the dense concentration of people in cities has resulted in a shortage of affordable housing.

2nd sentence gives a specific example or explains the problem in more detail.

Write here, then check the example answer below.

....

Example Answer

In several large cities, for example, a large number of people end up living in the suburbs since the shortage of space means renting in the city is too expensive.

The 3rd and 4th sentences give solutions to the issue.

Write here, then check the example answer below.

....

Example Answer

As a first step, governments should provide more affordable housing in city centers. UK cities like Manchester and London, for example, have government housing near the city centers to assist low-income families.

So the whole first body paragraph would be:

Firstly, the dense concentration of people in cities has resulted in a shortage of affordable housing. In several large cities, for example, a large number of people end up living in the suburbs since the shortage of space means renting in the city is too expensive. As a first step, governments should provide more affordable housing in city centers. UK cities like Manchester and London, for example, have government housing near the city centers to assist low-income families.

Body Paragraph 2

The second issue + solution…

1st sentence connects the previous paragraph to this new paragraph and presents the new issue.

Write here, then check the example answer on the next page.

………………………………………………………………

Example Answer

Living far away from work forces people to commute on a daily basis, which contributes to the second issue, traffic congestion.

We then use an example to offer a solid, realistic basis for our argument:

Write here, then check the example answer below.

....

Example Answer

Traffic congestion has become a critical issue in several cities worldwide. In Shanghai, for example, if you want to go from the East to the West, you may end up spending seven hours sitting in your car due to traffic jams.

Finally, we offer a solution and then explain why this is an important issue and why it needs solving… ('because it affects the quality of life)

Write here, then check the example answer below.

…………………………………………………………

Example Answer

Something governments must improve, is transportation infrastructure, in order to manage traffic volume. Many people commute on a daily basis, so having efficient public transport is crucial in order to improve quality of life.

The whole paragraph would look like this:

Living far away from work forces people to commute on a daily basis, which contributes to the second issue, traffic congestion. Traffic congestion has become a critical issue in several cities worldwide. In Shanghai, for example, if you want to go from the East to the West, you may end up spending seven hours sitting in your car due to traffic jams. Something governments must improve is transportation infrastructure in order to manage traffic volume. Many people commute on a daily basis, so having efficient public transport is crucial in order to improve quality of life.

Body Paragraph 3

In this final body paragraph, we discuss the third issue and solution in the same way as we did with the other two body paragraphs...

Write here, then check the example answer below.

....

Example Answer

Overpopulation and excessive traffic lead to pollution, which is the third issue to be addressed. As a result of the high population density in cities, air and water pollution issues are more prominent than in rural areas. This can lead to numerous health risks and can reduce quality of life. Local governments could encourage residents to be more mindful of the environment through events and information campaigns, for instance. Another possible solution is the implementation of car-free zones. This initiative has already been launched in several major cities worldwide, and it has had a significant impact on air quality.

Conclusion

Summarize the general topic:

Write here, then check the example answer below. Start your sentence with "*In summary,*…"

……………………………………………………………

Example Answer

In summary, population growth in cities around the world is causing several issues.

Summarize solutions:

Write here, then check the example answer below.

……………………………………………………………

Example Answer

To address them, we should do everything we can to offer affordable housing in urban areas, improve transportation, and make people aware of the impact that our lifestyle can have on the environment.

Special Vocabulary from the Example

- *Moving= relocating*

- *A better life= better quality of life*

- *housing shortages= a lack of suitable housing*

- *potential solutions= possible fixes*

- *dense concentration of people= overpopulation*

- *on a daily basis= daily = every day*

- *excessive traffic= too much traffic = traffic congestion*

- *the third issue to be addressed= To address an issue*

- *car-free zones = no-car zones*

Chapter 14. Discussion Essay

Typical Question Phrase:

➢ "Discuss both opinions and give your view."

Full Task Example:

Some people believe that single-sex schools are more beneficial to students because they achieve better academic results. Others, however, argue that mixed schools are better since students can develop better social skills.

Discuss both views and give your own opinion.

Tactics:

- Write about both sides

- Give a clear opinion

- It doesn't matter what your opinion is, as long as it's clear.

- It's important that your opinion is consistent with what you have written. This means that **it must be a logical opinion based on what you have evaluated.**

General Structure

Introduction

- Paraphrase Question and/or state both viewpoints.

- Let the examiner know what you will write about in the main body paragraphs (also called an 'outline sentence')

- Give your main opinion in one sentence (also called 'thesis statement').

Body Paragraph 1

1. State first viewpoint

2. Discuss the first viewpoint with example if applicable

Body Paragraph 2

1. State second viewpoint

2. Discuss the second viewpoint with an example if applicable.

Body Paragraph 3

1. The reason why you agree or disagree with one viewpoint

2. Example or argument to support your view

3. The reason why you agree or disagree with the other viewpoint.

4. Example or argument to support your opinion.

Conclusion

Sentence 1- Give a summary of your essay here

Sentence 2- Say which side of the argument you agree with

Common Mistakes

These are the most common mistakes that students make in IELTS discussion essays.

- **Not stating your opinion clearly enough so that the examiner understands it.**

- **Not writing about both sides of the argument.**

- **Not giving both sides of the argument equal attention.**

How To Plan IELTS Discussion Essays

Step 1: Analyze the question

This is a crucial part of the planning process and will help you answer the question properly and get an advanced grade (Bands 7-9).

The secret is to identify three different types of words:

- General Topic words

- Subtopic words

- Instruction words

Let's analyze the following exam question from the start of the chapter:

Some people believe that single-sex schools are more beneficial to students because they achieve better academic results. Others, however, argue that mixed schools are better since students can develop better social skills.

Discuss both views and give your own opinion.

Topic words: describe the general subject of the question. Some people believe that **single-sex schools** are more beneficial to students because they achieve better academic results. Others, however, argue that **mixed schools** are better since students can develop better social skills.

So, the question is about 'single-sex and mixed schools.'

Many IELTS candidates write about the topic in general when they get this type of essay in the test. This is wrong.

We have to identify <u>what sub-topic</u> related to 'single-sex and mixed schools' the examiner wants us to write about.

Subtopic words in the question tell us the exact topic we need to focus on.

"Some people believe that **single-sex schools are more beneficial to students because they achieve better academic results**. Others, however, argue that **mixed schools are better since students can develop better social skills**."

By identifying these words, we see that we're being asked about two opposite opinions. These two opinions are that single-sex schools are more beneficial to students because they achieve better academic results and that mixed schools are better since students often develop better social skills. Your essay needs to focus only on these subtopics.

Instruction words: As we've already looked at in previous essays, instruction words are the actual question words that we will be paraphrasing. In the case of the example above, the instruction words are:

"Discuss both views and give your own opinion."

Step 2: Decide on your opinion

Take the easiest opinion to write about!

The examiner doesn't care if you actually agree with the views you express in your essay or not. They care about the level of English you show. You will not be evaluated on any opinion you express, as long as it's expressed logically and in a well-structured manner.

So, choose your opinion and make sure it's clear throughout your essay.

In this example, we are going to say that mixed schools are better.

Introduction

Essay Question:

Some people believe that single-sex schools are more beneficial to students because they achieve better academic results. Others, however, argue that mixed schools are better since students can develop better social skills.

Discuss both views and give your own opinion.

Plan:

1. Paraphrase Question and/or state both viewpoints.

2. Let the examiner know what you will write about in the main body paragraphs (also called an 'outline sentence').

3. Your main opinion in one sentence (also called 'thesis statement')

Exercise

1st - Paraphrase the Issue:

Write a sentence to paraphrase the issue.

....

Example Answer

There is an ongoing debate as to whether the advantages of single-sex schools *outweigh the advantages of* mixed schools.

2nd Tell the examiner what you will discuss in the main body paragraphs

Write below:

....

Example Answer

While proponents of single-sex schools argue that children achieve better academic results when learning with their own gender, ***many people believe that*** mixed schools help **sharpen** children's social skills **to a higher degree**.

3rd – Give Opinion

Write below:

....

Example Answer

Although both sides make very valid points, I would argue that mixed schools are better for most children, since they offer.

Therefore, the introduction paragraph will look like this:

There is an ongoing debate as to whether the advantages of single-sex schools outweigh the advantages of mixed schools. While proponents of single-sex schools argue that children achieve better academic results when learning with their own gender, many people believe that mixed schools help sharpen children's social skills to a higher degree. Although both sides make very valid points, I would argue that mixed schools are better for most children.

Body Paragraph 1

Plan:

1. State first viewpoint

2. Discuss the first viewpoint with example if applicable

This 1st sentence connects back to the question and signals what we arc going to talk about.

Write below. Start with "*On the one hand.*"

....

Example Answer

<u>On the one hand, it could be argued that</u> mixed schools offer a more natural environment where students can learn side-by-side with the opposite sex.

Discuss the first viewpoint with an example if applicable

Write below:

....

Example Answer

__This way__, children can learn to interact and collaborate with their peers **regardless of** *gender. This often creates healthier long-term relations with people of the opposite gender.* **__Furthermore, it is often claimed that__** *mixed schools can provide students with improved* **conflict management skills.** *They are more likely to be exposed to* a **broader range** *of opinions* **regarding** *social, political, and gender issues.* **They will, in theory,** *learn* **to better manage** *disagreements with both genders.*

Therefore, the first body paragraph will look like this....

On the one hand, it could be argued that mixed schools offer a more natural environment where students can learn side-by-side with the opposite sex. This way, children can learn to interact and collaborate with their peers regardless of gender. This often creates healthier long-term relations with people of the opposite gender. Furthermore, it is often claimed that mixed schools can provide students with improved conflict management skills. They are more likely to be exposed to a broader range of opinions regarding social, political, and gender issues. They will, in theory, learn to better manage disagreements with both genders.

Body Paragraph 2

Plan:

1. State second viewpoint

2. Discuss the second viewpoint with an example if applicable.

State the second viewpoint in one sentence.

Start with *"On the other hand"*:

Write below:

....

Example Answer

<u>*On the other hand, in some cases,*</u> *single-sex schools have fewer distractions* <u>**and will therefore**</u> *produce better academic results.*

Discuss the second viewpoint with an example if applicable.

Write below:

....

Example Answer

This has actually been proven in some schools, and it is definitely something worth considering. Students who achieve higher grades will often go on to become more successful in life, leading to **greater prosperity,** *in many cases, and* **greater career satisfaction.**

Body Paragraph 3

Give your opinion here...

Plan:

1. The reason why you agree or disagree with the first or second viewpoint

2. Example or argument to support your view

3. The reason why you agree or disagree with the first or second viewpoint.

4. Example or argument to support your view

Outline a reason why you disagree with the argument in favor of single-sex schools.

Start with "*However, in my opinion...*"

Write below:

....

Example Answer

__However, in my opinion,__ students can be equally distracted by members of the opposite sex, __regardless of whether__ they are physically present in the classroom __or not__.

Example or argument to support your view

Write below:

....

Example Answer

Students cannot avoid interacting with members of the other sex in their everyday lives. ***Therefore, it seems counterintuitive to*** *segregate them in school.*

Outline the reason why you agree with the argument in favor of mixed schools.

Write below. Start with *"An added benefit of mixed schools is…"*:

....

Example Answer

An added benefit of mixed schools is that they
enable students to interact and co-exist with the other gender in a real-
life environment…

Example or argument to support your view.

Write below:

···

Example Answer

… where they can learn the personal boundaries that must be
respected, and they can develop a more profound sense of connection
and empathy.

Conclusion

Plan:

Sentence 1- Summary of the issue

Sentence 2- State which side of the discussion you agree with and why.

Summary

Start with *"In conclusion, I firmly believe that…"*

Write below:

....

Example Answer

In conclusion, I firmly believe *that developing superior social skills* ***is far more critical to overall long-term*** *success and happiness than academic achievement, especially during childhood. . It is also unrealistic to assume that we can eliminate natural distractions from the classroom.*

State which side of the discussion you agree with:

Write below:

....

Example Answer

__As a result,__ I agree with the proponents of mixed schools.

So, the whole conclusion paragraph can look like this:

__In conclusion, I firmly believe__ that developing superior social skills is __far more critical to overall long-term__ success and happiness than academic achievement, especially during childhood. . It is also unrealistic to assume that we can eliminate natural distractions from the classroom. __As a result,__ I agree with the proponents of mixed schools.

Special Vocabulary

Sharpen children's social skills to a higher degree

children can learn to interact and collaborate with their peers regardless of gender.

Improved conflict management skills.

A broader range of opinions regarding social, political, and gender issues.

They will, in theory,...

greater prosperity

greater career satisfaction

Give your opinion…

regardless of whether they are physically present in the classroom or not.

it seems counterintuitive to segregate them in school

they enable students to interact and co-exist

personal boundaries

a more profound sense of connection and empathy

Chapter 15. Two-Part Essay Question

Full Question Example:

This type of essay asks you to answer TWO questions.

Nowadays, people eat food from different parts of the world, not only local food. What do you think is driving this habit? Is this a good or bad development? Give reasons for your answer and include any relevant examples from your own knowledge or experience.

General Structure

You can plan your essay as follows:

Introduction:

1- Paraphrase the first part of the question to summarize the general topic.

2- Write a sentence to tell the examiner what you will write about.

Body Paragraph 1

1- Answer 1st question

2- Give a realistic example(s) with a world view

Body Paragraph 2

1- Answer 2nd question

2- Give a realistic example(s) with a world view

Conclusion

1- Sentence 1- Summary of reasons for your opinion

2- Sentence 2- State opinion clearly again.

Common Mistakes

- Not completely answering both questions.

- Not identifying both answers in the essay introduction.

Brainstorming Ideas

Let's look at an example of how you could plan this essay.

Nowadays, an increasing number of young people are using the Internet to socialize.

What do you think is driving this habit?

You Only Need One or Two Ideas!

- You only need one or two ideas!

- There is a lot of information to write about this topic, so we need to make sure that we keep our writing under control here!

- We have TWO questions to answer, not one!

- Choose one main idea for each question.

- Choose ideas that are easy to think of examples for.

Examples of Ideas for this Topic:

- Pandemic

- Teleworking, online banking, etc. Our lives are more and more online, so why not socialize online?

- Lack of time

- Less emphasis on social skills and more emphasis on technology at school?

- The emergence of social media has made it more and more acceptable to socialize online

Do you believe this is positive or negative?

- Neither positive nor negative, it needs to be controlled.

- Cyberbullying

Introduction

Plan:

- Paraphrase the issue

- Outline sentence – give your answer to both questions (a sentence to tell the examiner what you will write about)

Question:

Nowadays, an increasing number of young people are using the Internet to socialize.

What do you think is driving this habit? Do you believe this is positive or negative? Give reasons for your answer and include any relevant examples from your own knowledge or experience.

Exercise

1st - Paraphrase the Issue

2nd – Write a sentence to tell the examiner what you will write about.

Write the full introduction below:

....

Example Answer

So, the full introduction looks like this on paper:

At present, there are increasingly more people under the age of thirty who are turning to the Internet to socialize. This essay will discuss two of the main driving forces behind this behavior and the main reasons why I believe it is mostly a negative trend.

Body Paragraph 1

Plan:

1- Answer 1st question

2- Give a realistic example(s) with a world view

Write below:

Firstly, it is reasonable to assume that ....

Example Answer

The full-body paragraph looks like this on paper:

Firstly, it is reasonable to assume that one of the main driving forces behind the rise in online socializing is the advent of social media in the last two decades. Digital natives have grown up being able to communicate with people from all over the world through direct messages, photographs, voice chat, and video. This has arguably shaped the way they interact and has shifted more of their social connections online. In addition to the influence of social media, young people have had to deal with unprecedented situations, such as the 2008 financial crisis or the more recent COVID-19 pandemic. While the 2008 financial crisis led to many young people being unable to find work and spending extended periods of time at home, the COVID-19 pandemic left much of the world's population effectively house-bound for weeks and in some cases, months on end. This meant that people had to adapt, as they had to do all of their socializing online.

Body Paragraph 2

Plan:

1st Answer 2nd question

Reason 1 for opinion

Reason 2 for opinion

2nd Give a realistic example(s) with a world view

A real-world example for Reason 1

A real-world example for Reason 2

Write your Body Paragraph 2 below:

. . . .

Example Answer

Although there are many benefits to socializing online, and it has proven to be highly advantageous in extreme situations such as the pandemic, it is mostly a negative trend when it is overused, in my opinion. For starters, cyberbullying is a major threat to the well-being of both children and adolescents. Cyberbullying occurs on a regular basis on platforms such as Instagram and Facebook, and the rate of suicide among teenagers is arguably on the rise as a result of this phenomenon. Another issue is young people who socialize online have fewer opportunities to practice their interpersonal skills. Users are increasingly texting one another on Facebook and WhatsApp rather than socializing in person. This can lead to anti-social behaviors and depression, as they lose real social connections and feel increasingly isolated.

Conclusion

Plan:

1- Sentence 1- Summary of reasons for your opinion

2- Sentence 2- State opinion clearly again.

Write your conclusion below:

....

Example Answer

So, the conclusion paragraph looks like this on paper:

In conclusion, socializing online, if overused, can affect young people's mental health as well as their quality of life. This is why I believe that online socializing is mostly detrimental.

Special Vocabulary

there are increasingly more people

under the age of thirty

turning to the internet to socialize.

the main driving forces

a negative trend

it is reasonable to assume that

the advent of social media in the last two decades

Digital natives

has shifted more of their social connections online

In addition to the influence of social media,

unprecedented situations

extended periods of time

effectively house-bound

for weeks, and in some cases, months on end

wellbeing

Marc Roche

Cyberbullying occurs on a regular basis

is arguably on the rise as a result of this phenomenon

mostly detrimental

Chapter 16. Essay Phrase Bank

Useful Phrases

- I do not feel this is a direct cause of…

- Of course, it goes without saying that…

- There has been a growing body of opinion that…

- … the situation can be addressed by adopting the methods mentioned above…

- While I admit that… I would argue that…

- One approach would be…

- A second possibility would be to…

- Obviously,…

- However,

- This suggests that…

- In addition,…

- To sum up…

- In fact…

- I tend to disagree…

- I am unconvinced by…

- Overall,…

- In the final analysis…

- Ultimately,…

- To conclude…

- In conclusion…

- On the other hand,…

- There is no doubt that…

- This could involve…

- Thirdly…

Expressing Views

- I would argue that…

- I firmly believe that…

- It seems to me that...

- I tend to think that…

- People argue that...

- Some people think that…

- Many people feel that…

- In my experience…

- It is undoubtedly true that...

- It is certainly true that….

Refuting an Argument

- I am unconvinced that...

- I do not believe that...

- It I hard to accept that...

- It is unjustifiable to say that...

    - There is little evidence to support that...

Providing Support

- For example,...

- For instance,...

- Indeed,...

- In fact,...

- Of course,...

- It can be generally observed that...

- Statistics demonstrate...

- If this is/were the case...

- Firstly,...

- Naturally,…

- In my experience…

- Let me illustrate…

Defining and Explaining

- I would argue that…

- By this I mean…

- In other words...

- This is to say…

- To be more precise...

- Here I am referring to …

Use These Carefully

- First/second, etc.…

- Moreover...

- In addition,…

- Furthermore,…

- Nevertheless/nonetheless…

- On the one/other hand…

- Besides…

- Consequently...

- In contrast...

- In comparison...

Use Moderately

- While...

- Meanwhile...

- Although...

- In spite of.../ Despite the fact that...

- Even though...

- As a result,...

- However,...

- Since...

- Similarly,...

- Thus...

- In turn

Other Useful Phrases

- My response to this argument depends on what is meant by...

- There is surely a difference between.... and....

- I intend to illustrate how some of these differences are significant to the argument put forward.

- However, whilst I agree that... I am less convinced that...

- I certainly believe that...

- One of the main arguments in favor of.... is that...

- In other words,...

- Admittedly, in some ways...

- Surely...

- Arguably...

- Either way...

- In any case...

- The most important point is that...

- Another point is that...

- Of crucial importance, in my opinion, is...

- There is, however, another possible way of defining...

- ...that I am in favor of, although I also realize that...

- Therefore...

- There is no doubt that...

- However, it is possible to tackle this serious issue in a number of ways.

- One approach would be...

- ...would be particularly beneficial.

- A second possibility would be to...

- ...this could involve...

- Many people feel that this is unacceptable because...

- Opponents of... point out that ... and argue that...

- On the other hand, it cannot be denied that...

- Supporters of...argue that...

Introducing a False Argument

- It could be argued that...

- Some people would argue that...

- There is also the idea implicit in the statement that...

- It is often suggested that...

Destroying a False Argument

- This is partly true, but...

- To a certain extent, there is some truth in this..., however,...

- However, the implication that... is an oversimplification.

- This argument has certain specific logic, but…

Suggesting a Correct Argument

- It is clear that…

- The real situation…

- Obviously…

- On the contrary…

- It is therefore quite wrong to suggest that…

Chapter 17. IELTS Essay Templates

Use these sample essays to review and refresh functional language and structures for high band score IELTS essays without memorizing them.

Instead, please pay close attention to how they are written to internalize the language, structure, and style.

Read, make notes, and review as much as possible to get the most benefit from this book. This is one of the most effective ways to raise your IELTS writing band score.

While you read these sample essays, think about how you can incorporate these sentence structures into your writing.

Many students find it helpful to paraphrase sentences that they like from the essay or write example sentences using the language from the essay.

Essay Template 1

Some people believe that single-sex schools are more beneficial to students because they achieve better academic results. Others, however, argue that mixed schools are better since students can develop better social skills.

Discuss both views and give your own opinion.

There is an ongoing debate as to whether the advantages of single-sex schools **outweigh the advantages of** mixed schools. **While proponents of** single-sex schools argue that children achieve better academic results when learning with their own gender, **many people believe that** mixed schools help **sharpen** children's social skills **to a higher degree.** Although both sides make very valid points, I would argue that mixed schools are better for most children.

On the one hand, it could be argued that mixed schools offer a more natural environment where students can learn side-by-side with the opposite sex. This way, children can learn to interact and collaborate with their peers **regardless of** gender. This often creates healthier long-term relations with people of the opposite gender. **Furthermore, it is often claimed that** mixed schools can provide students with improved conflict management skills. They are more likely to be exposed to a **broader range** of opinions **regarding** social, political, and gender issues. **They will, in theory,** learn **to better manage** disagreements with both genders.

On the other hand, in some cases, single-sex schools have fewer distractions **and will therefore** produce better academic results. This has actually been proven in some schools, and it is definitely something worth considering. Students who achieve higher grades will often go on to become more successful in life, leading to greater prosperity, in many cases, and greater career satisfaction.

However, in my opinion, students can be equally distracted by members of the opposite sex, **regardless of whether** they are physically present in the classroom **or not.** Students cannot avoid interacting with members of the other sex in their everyday lives. **Therefore, it seems counterintuitive** to segregate them in school. **An added benefit of** mixed schools is that they **enable** students **to** interact and co-exist with the other gender in a real-life environment where they can learn the personal boundaries that must be respected, and they can develop a more profound sense of connection and empathy.

In conclusion, I firmly believe that developing superior social skills is **far more critical to overall long-term** success and happiness than academic achievement, especially during childhood. **As a result,** I agree with the proponents of mixed schools.

Essay Template 2

Some employers think that job candidates' social skills are more important than their academic qualifications.

Do you agree or disagree?

There is ongoing discussion about whether interpersonal skills are more important than academic achievement **when it comes to** employee success. **While I partially agree that** social skills **are often** a more accurate indicator of employee performance than academic qualifications alone, I also believe that **this is not always the case.**

Firstly, it is reasonable to assume that communication skills are central to most, if not all, jobs nowadays, as most positions require constant interaction with colleagues and clients. Furthermore, with the emergence of social media and other online communication tools, people are arguably interacting more than ever. **This increased level of interaction** makes it even more crucial for employees to excel in their communication.

Secondly, networking is **arguably a significant part** of employee success in all jobs, whether client-facing or technical. **For example,** employees with excellent interpersonal skills **are more likely to** contribute to a collaborative and productive atmosphere within their company. They also tend to project their company positively when dealing with external stakeholders, strengthening their brand image.

Research suggests that positive work environments **lead to** higher levels of productivity and happiness throughout departments and companies as a whole. This often leads to greater employee retention and higher profitability in the long term, as staff members tend to be happier and more settled in their jobs.

Nevertheless, there are specific jobs where academic or practical qualifications are essential for carrying out the work. Doctors, nurses, engineers, police officers, and many other professionals need to hold the necessary qualifications to prove they have the technical knowledge and practical training to work in their field.

I believe both social skills and academic qualifications **have a role to play. While it is probably true**

to say that social skills are the most crucial factor for long-term success and happiness, academic qualifications are often the minimum requirement to carry out certain jobs. Therefore, it would be wise for most employers to seek a balance of both.

Essay Template 3

According to some people, students from all economic backgrounds should be able to attend university. They believe that the government should provide free university education for everyone.

Do you agree with this opinion?

The question of whether or not the government should consider making tertiary education available to all learners has been the subject of recent public discussion. Higher education**, in my opinion,** should be free regardless of income, based on the grounds that it would benefit both individuals and society.

Firstly, one argument in favor of eliminating university fees is that there are many learners who are unable to pay for their education, despite their strong desire to obtain degrees. Without sufficient financial support, these students have no other way to fulfill their dreams. Even in cases where students can afford to pay for university, they often have to take out loans and work part-time to pay for their living costs. This can severely affect their grades, and therefore, their future career development. It can also leave them with large debts to pay when they finish studying. **These financial barriers** may discourage highly talented students from pursuing a university education.

Secondly, no country can prosper without an educated population, so funding free university education is a long-term investment into the future of the country. Taxpayers' money **is arguably** being **misused** by the government on initiatives like space exploration. If a country can't educate its population, there is no sense in investing large amounts of money into ambitious space projects. A far more sensible distribution of government funds could allow thousands of students to fulfill their dreams. This would lead to a more educated society, which would, no doubt, benefit the country as a whole for many years (to come).

In conclusion, free university education, regardless of income, is crucial for **any society seeking sustainable progress**. Expensive tuition fees may discourage some individuals from pursuing university degrees, as young people are often unwilling to carry the burden of their loans for many years after graduation, making university less appealing. The government should be responsible for the cost of tertiary education. Hence, it would be appropriate for the government to distribute financial resources better in order to do this.

Essay Template 4

Several languages have become extinct as time goes on. However, this might potentially make our lives easier since there will be fewer languages to learn.

Do you agree with this statement?

At a time when everything is changing rapidly, English as a universal language enables cross-cultural interaction. This means that many languages become extinct each year, which some people do not consider to be important, as they believe that life without so many languages will be easier. I do not agree with this view, as I believe it has a negative impact on the cultural identities of millions of people around the world, and it leads to cultural loss.

Several issues have arisen as a result of the extinction of minority languages. Firstly, the spread of the English language threatens to destroy the cultural identities of people of other ethnicities. More precisely, the widespread use of English can exacerbate the feeling of cultural inferiority of those who speak languages that are less popular.

Secondly, when other languages fade, we also experience a loss of culture. For example, Latin is a defunct language since, at present, almost nobody can speak it. Hence, the culture that supports Latin has almost disappeared. When cultural loss takes place, the extinction of cultural heritage, including traditional values, also occurs. Several important values, such as family and education, are greatly regarded in some cultures, and hence, losing those cultures would threaten those values.

To summarize, while English is a language that allows for cross-cultural interaction, other languages are just as important. I truly believe that non-English languages should be treated with respect and that they should be safeguarded and preserved.

Essay Template 5

The law should be changed to protect historic buildings, according to some people. Other people believe that change in this area is always positive and that new buildings should replace the old ones.

Analyze and express your thoughts on both of these points of view.

In today's society, numerous cities are confronted with **the question of whether or not to** demolish old buildings and construct new ones in their place. As far as I'm concerned, old buildings must be preserved, as they are part of our cultural heritage and history. Furthermore, historic buildings provide the financial benefits associated with increased tourism.

To begin with, historic buildings such as Big Ben, the Pantheon, or Himeji Castle **are of immense value, as** they are associated with specific historical events or figures. More precisely, if such structures were demolished, the respective events and figures would no longer be accurately represented. Moreover, some old buildings are part of ethnic groups' unique cultures. **Should these** buildings **be** demolished, **it may result in** an ethnological catastrophe. Many historical buildings possess exceptional aesthetic qualities. No replication can truly represent the original craftsmanship.

With the fast increase in the city's population, it is inevitable that certain historic buildings will be demolished in order to provide the space needed to build new apartments. However, it would be far more practical to simply improve public transportation, allowing commuters to travel to work from nearby suburbs. Demolishing historic buildings would **undoubtedly lead to** a loss of tourists. This, **in turn,** would lead to **considerable financial loss** for the area **in question.**

To summarize, old buildings may take up a lot of space, but their importance should not be overlooked. I believe that modern cities have a responsibility to preserve historic buildings. It is also **very much** in their interest **from an** economic **standpoint.**

Essay Template 6

Global tourism has grown to be a multibillion-dollar industry. Some believe that the problems of international tourism outweigh its benefits.

Do you agree?

International tourism is a huge industry that provides millions of jobs worldwide. Although there are many benefits and problems associated with international tourism, **I personally believe** that the advantages clearly outweigh the disadvantages. **Not only does it** provide excellent learning opportunities and cultural exchange, **but it also** boosts local economies and improves the quality of life.

There are numerous advantages to international tourism that can be enjoyed at various levels. For example, it provides individuals with first-hand opportunities to explore other cultures. Traveling to a different country, in my opinion, is a much more **enriching experience** than simply learning about other cultures online. **In addition,** the knowledge gained from international travel can undoubtedly assist in eliminating a variety of stereotypes that people may have about the country they are visiting. Individuals can broaden their horizons and gain a more global perspective on life.

Furthermore, international tourism contributes to the growth of the economy. Australia, for example, has experienced a boom in international tourism over the past few years, which has created a variety of job opportunities across the country. In many regions, the local economy is dependent on tourism, so if it disappeared, it would **severely affect**

people's livelihood, leading to poverty and **an overall loss** of quality of life.

It goes without saying that tourists' non-biodegradable waste is a considerable threat to the host nation. However, it is certainly possible for tourist destinations to lay down legislation and regulations to address this problem. Once international tourism has had a positive impact on the economy of the host nation, the local government can easily put in place effective strategies to address the issue.

In brief, despite the fact that the environment of tourist destinations **may be negatively affected**, the advantages of tourism outweigh the disadvantages. International tourism is a fantastic way for people to learn about other cultures, and many regions are **economically dependent on** it. This has **a hugely positive impact on** the quality of life and overall happiness in many regions across the globe.

Essay Template 7

People differ on whether or not public health is the government's responsibility, with some believing that people should take care of their own healthcare treatments, while others think the government is responsible for it.

What is your opinion?

The question of whether public health is the responsibility of the government or the responsibility of individuals has sparked a debate in today's society. Public health, in my opinion, should be the responsibility of each individual **first and foremost**. I believe that the role of the government should be limited, as it is not feasible or fair to expect it to effectively manage the healthcare of millions of people with individual needs and lifestyle choices.

For a variety of reasons, individuals are expected to take responsibility for their own health. **To begin with,** people are more knowledgeable about their own health than anyone else. **Given that** the government is unable to comprehend the needs of everyone in a realistic manner, it is incumbent upon individuals to assume responsibility for their own well-being. In my opinion, it is simply not possible for a government to adequately cater to the healthcare of millions of people who each have individual needs and lifestyles.

In addition, the ability to exercise self-control, and manage your lifestyle, is essential for good health. **Nobody would dispute the fact that** poor lifestyle choices often lead to illnesses and poor general health. **I, therefore, believe** that individuals should have private insurance that covers their medical bills instead of forcing society to cover the expense.

Finally, the government must provide adequate support in order to improve public health outcomes. **However, I believe** that **this** support **should be in the form of** high-quality education and information services that will allow individuals to manage their health more adequately. People must take personal responsibility for their own well-being because the government will never be able to take care of everyone's needs. If people receive adequate information and education, they will be able to make independent choices to improve their lifestyles. **This will arguably break the cycle** of unhealthy lifestyles and poor health, improving public health **in the long term.**

In conclusion, society as a whole cannot be expected to pay for the individual lifestyle choices that we all make and that affect our long-term health. I believe that public health is not the government's financial responsibility but that the government should play a supporting role through the provision of education and information services.

Essay Template 8

When individuals with cultural differences work and live together, they are said to be living in a multicultural society.

Do you believe that the advantages of living in a multicultural society outweigh the disadvantages?

The question of whether the benefits of living in a multicultural society outweigh the drawbacks **has been sparking debate for several years.** I believe that having individuals with different cultural backgrounds work and live together **is beneficial on many levels** and that, therefore, the advantages outweigh the disadvantages.

A variety of advantages are created by living and working in a diverse society. **For starters,** multicultural environments allow people to broaden their understanding of the world and human nature. Different cultures produce different perspectives and ideas, which help people learn more about the world. Having people from different parts of the world living together in the same region can provide excellent learning opportunities, as people are exposed to various languages, cultures, and traditions. People can experience different foods and customs every day, leading to more tolerance and improved relations among communities.

Furthermore, individuals from a variety of cultural backgrounds benefit society in many other ways. Because of their multicultural nature, countries like Australia, the UK, and

Canada run various yearly events to celebrate the coming together of different cultures. These festivals **serve as** tourist attractions that boost the local economy, providing jobs and prosperity. These celebrations have the added effect of solidifying the area's identity and uniting people in celebration, which arguably contributes to a healthier, happier society.

One potential stumbling block is if the situation is not managed correctly and new communities do not integrate. **This can lead to** a feeling of isolation which often causes conflict and resentment if not managed properly. Furthermore, suppose communities become entrenched in specific areas within a city, and there are insufficient resources to serve all communities equally. In that case, **this can result in** further conflict as a feeling of injustice becomes widespread.

After considering all of the points made above, I do not see any significant disadvantages to living in a multicultural environment, provided the situation is managed correctly and all communities are fully integrated. **I am confident that, in theory,** the advantages outweigh the disadvantages **from both an** economic and a cultural **standpoint.** Furthermore, to develop as a society and prosper in the long term, **we must foster** an atmosphere of respect and tolerance among cultures. Cultural diversity can enrich society on many levels and force us to confront our prejudices.

Essay Template 9

Subjects should only be offered in schools if they improve students' future careers. There is no need to offer subjects such as art, sports, and music.

Do you agree with this statement?

There is currently a discussion as to whether schools should only teach subjects that can aid people to succeed in their career prospects. **This implies** that subjects such as music and sports are not worth offering since, for most students, they do not directly offer many career prospects. **I genuinely think** that studying music and taking up sports are just as important.

Firstly, students who participate in art, music, and sports receive a broader education. Although most students may not work in music or sports, having a broad education that includes subjects like these can provide them with greater creativity and better physical and mental health. These qualities can significantly influence someone's level of success in their career and personal life. **There is also evidence to suggest that** children and adolescents who are artistic and athletic are much more prone to being in good physical and mental shape **in their old age.** This is extremely important for quality of life, and it should not be overlooked.

Besides that, subjects such as music, sports, and art assist learners in identifying their interests and hobbies at an early age in their education. Finding out what you are truly passionate about at a young age will allow you to carry that passion into adulthood. **It is crucial to remember that** arts, sports, and music assist students in finding a balance in their academic learning. It goes without saying that if students only learn English and mathematics at school, their lives will be extremely monotonous. Having a healthy balance **can** improve overall student performance, leading to greater career prospects.

Mainstream society has **a very narrow definition** of what it means to be successful. **The vast majority of** individuals think that they can only achieve success if they can make more money. **However, a more in-depth examination would reveal that,** in the long run, being happy is almost certainly more important than being rich. Therefore, **I firmly believe** that music, art, and sports are just as important as English and math and that they should all be taught at school.

Essay Template 10

<u>**Two-Part Question Essay Version:**</u>

Nowadays, an increasing number of young people are using the internet to socialize.

What do you think is driving this habit? Do you believe this is positive or negative? Give reasons for your answer and include any relevant examples from your own knowledge or experience.

At present, there are **increasingly** more people **under the age of thirty** who are **turning to** the Internet to socialize. This essay will discuss two of the main driving forces behind this behavior and the main reasons why I believe it is mostly a negative trend.

Firstly, it is reasonable to assume that one of the main driving forces behind the rise in online socializing is the **advent** of social media in the last two decades. Digital natives have grown up being able to communicate with people worldwide through direct messages, photographs, voice chat, and video. This has arguably shaped the way they interact and has shifted more of their social connections online. In addition to the influence of social media, young people have had to deal with unprecedented situations, such as the 2008 financial crisis or the more recent COVID-19 pandemic. While the 2008 financial crisis led to many young people being unable to find work and spending extended periods at home, the COVID-19 pandemic left much of the world's population effectively house-bound for weeks and in some cases, months on end. This meant that people had to adapt, as they had to do all of their socializing online.

Although there are many advantages to socializing online, and it has proven to be highly advantageous in extreme situations such as the pandemic, it is mostly a negative trend when it is overused, in my opinion. **For starters,** cyberbullying is a major threat to the well-being of both children and adolescents. Cyberbullying **occurs on a regular basis** on platforms such as Instagram and Facebook, and the rate of suicide among teenagers **is arguably on the rise as a result of this phenomenon. Another issue is that** young people who socialize online have fewer opportunities to practice their interpersonal skills. Users are increasingly texting one another on Facebook and WhatsApp rather than socializing in person. This can lead to anti-social behaviors and depression, as they lose real social connections and feel increasingly isolated.

In conclusion, if overused, socializing online can affect young people's mental health and quality of life. This is why I believe that online socializing is mostly **detrimental.**

Essay Template 11

When studying a foreign language, students should learn about the culture and lifestyles behind that language.

Do you agree with this statement?

Many students nowadays study foreign languages. However, **the question of whether** students should also be taught about the culture behind that language **has turned into a hotly disputed topic in recent years**. **I mostly agree** that foreign languages should be learned along with their culture. **For the reasons listed below,** I believe that, **to a certain extent,** it is necessary to learn both the language and culture simultaneously.

First and foremost, language and culture are **inextricably linked**. **Many studies have found that** learning a new language without understanding its culture is deceptive, as the language is supported by its culture. Moreover, learning about other cultures makes learning a foreign language more enjoyable. Learning a new language is not simple. Incorporating the cultural component into the learning process will make it more engaging. Culture is vital when it comes to long-term learning. Exploring cultures while learning a new foreign language is what turns learners into bilinguals.

However, learning about a new culture **can, at times, be** distracting **when it comes to** foreign language education. Dedicating too much time to studying the culture may result in losing focus from the primary objective, which is learning the language. Therefore, there should be a healthy balance between learning the language and learning about the culture and its history, in my opinion.

I believe that learning both culture and language is the most effective approach. Without comprehending a country's culture, parts of the language may be rendered incomprehensible. In many cases, learning about the culture can provide the foundation for mastering the language.

Essay Template 12

Nowadays, an increasing number of parents rely on their children's grandparents to care for them.

Do you believe this is a good or bad thing?

Several issues are unavoidably raised when children are cared for by their grandparents. These days, most parents are turning to their kids' grandparents to get help with childcare. I believe that this is a negative change.

Firstly, **it is crucial for** children **to** bond with their parents. The love between kids and their parents is usually unconditional. Therefore, not spending enough time with their parents can be extremely negative for children's development.

Furthermore, grandparents are typically older, **implying that** they are **less likely to** possess sufficient physical and mental energy to care for small children adequately. Childcare is a demanding task **that is not always suitable** for older people. A child's grandparents should enjoy their lives and freedom, so it is not fair to expect them to devote all of their spare time to child care.

Of course, I recognize that not all parents have the financial means or the time to care for their kids independently. In today's society, work and life can be demanding. Parents should, however, learn to prioritize their lives and enhance their family relationships.

In conclusion, I believe grandparents shouldn't take responsibility for childcare. Parents should care for their children, as this is not only the best option for everyone, but it is the right thing to do.

Essay Template 13

People are divided on whether or not the government should offer financial support for the arts. Some people think that the money should be used to improve public health and education programs.

Do you agree with this viewpoint?

The question of whether the government should spend money on the arts **or** public health and education **has sparked widespread public debate.** In my opinion, more financial resources should be allocated to health and education. Increased government funding for public health and education is unquestionably needed for various reasons.

Possibly the most important reason to consider is that health and education are necessary conditions for a happy, healthy society to function. Nobody would dispute that focusing on public health and education significantly lowers crime rates and that lower crime rates lead to increased quality of life. Offering further funding for healthcare and education would also lead to greater opportunities for young people and better life expectancy for people of all ages. Patients would receive better treatment from hospitals and healthcare centers.

Furthermore, while the arts are extremely important, **there is evidence to suggest that** the number of individuals who rely on government support in health care and education is increasing. As a result, the population's needs must be met first. If people's basic needs for education and healthcare are not met, they will not **be in the state of mind to** enjoy the arts.

I acknowledge that the arts are extremely important. Despite this, the government must prioritize the areas that need financial support to be effective. It is well understood that public health and education require greater financial support than the arts. Considering everything, I believe that the government **would be wise to** fund public health care and education for the population to be happy.

Essay Template 14

Certain people truly believe that planning for the future is a complete waste of time. They think that the present should be the focus.

Do you agree with this view?

Some people think that living for the moment and enjoying the present is more important than making plans for the future. In my opinion, a life without any planning for the future can be chaotic and stressful. So, while it is important to be present and enjoy the moment, a degree of planning is always required in order to live a full, happy life. There are numerous reasons to make plans for the future.

It is probably true to say that people who have goals generally understand what they want in life and, as a result, have more confidence in their decisions since they have usually thought them through and planned them. This leads to higher levels of long-term happiness and success in many cases. Never knowing what you need to do next or constantly making mistakes and forgetting important events can be highly stressful and severely affect your quality of life, as well as your long-term health.

Furthermore, making plans for the future provides people with motivation. Most individuals are motivated by a vision they have for their future. Making plans for the future renders a person's growth more feasible. It is true that even the most successful people can become distracted and discouraged at times. As a result, they may find it difficult to appreciate their accomplishments and enjoy their success fully. Having clearly defined goals can help minimize this issue.

Finally, a balanced lifestyle that includes specific and realistic goals, together with a healthy amount of focus on the present, is more likely to lead to long-term happiness and fulfillment. **There is evidence that suggests that** purposefully focusing on the present can be part of a healthy, balanced lifestyle. Practices such as mindfulness and meditation, for instance, have numerous reported benefits, such as reducing stress and even blood pressure.

In conclusion, I believe that developing a long-term strategy and concentrating on the present **are not mutually exclusive**. Concentrating on clear goals helps individuals to become more organized in their daily lives and happier overall. As a result, it would be better if people started planning for their futures as soon as possible without neglecting their short-term happiness and well-being.

Essay Template 15

A number of people believe that distance learning can take the place of traditional education.

Do you agree with this statement?

The internet is evolving at an incredible rate in today's society, thanks to the advancement of modern technologies. **There is disagreement, however, over whether** online education can take the place of formal education. Distance learning, in my opinion, will never be able to replace traditional education completely. In comparison to online education, schools provide a variety of benefits.

It is widely recognized that a person's communication skills are critical for personal and professional development in today's world. Students must learn such skills through exposure to real social situations. Therefore, traditional education alongside classmates and teachers is the most natural and effective way to improve their social skills. The importance of friendships established at school cannot be overlooked.

Teachers are also **more able to meet** the diverse needs of their students in the classroom, which is yet another benefit of face-to-face learning. Teachers who can see their students in class arguably find it a lot easier to recognize the students' needs and take appropriate action. This can prevent or solve issues connected to bullying, learning disabilities, or demotivation, for example. It would be extremely difficult for a teacher to monitor these issues and offer support online effectively.

To summarize, distance learning may have some advantages, but it will never completely replace traditional schooling. I am confident that traditional education will continue to help students in their personal and professional development in the future. By learning through traditional face-to-face education, students can improve their communication skills and lead a balanced, happy life.

Essay Template 16

Many older people often hold some traditional ideas on the correct way of life, thought and behavior. Many people argue that these traditional ideas are not helpful for younger generations in preparing for modern life.

To what extent do you agree or disagree?

There are differing opinions on whether the traditional values carried by previous generations can assist young people in adjusting to modern lifestyles. **I mostly disagree with the notion that** traditional values and cultural norms do not help younger generations to prepare for modern life. **I believe that**, while some may be unhelpful, many traditional values are still relevant today, despite many things having changed.

Numerous traditional values **still hold today**. For example, no matter what century it is, family is always an essential part of life. For the vast majority of people, the only place to find unconditional love is within their families. Another value that should continue to be highly regarded is honesty. Honesty and integrity are critical in today's society, where trust is at the core of everything we do. Having respect for others also continues to be crucial in today's society. No one can deny that being treated with respect is much more important than being liked.

Some old ideas, **on the other hand, may be considered** regressive. The fact that women are traditionally not regarded as high achievers in society serves as an example of what should be considered a regressive idea. This is a potentially damaging belief that we should disregard.

We should not discard all traditional values because they contain elements that date back to an antiquated era. The majority of traditional values should be loved, cherished, and respected by young people. They are timeless concepts that can serve as the foundation of their preparation for modern life.

Essay Template 17

Some people believe that using animals for the benefit of humankind is justifiable. Others believe that exploiting animals is simply wrong.

What's your view?

People have different opinions on whether or not exploiting animals for the benefit of humankind is justifiable. **However, I am a firm believer that** using animals is unethical. The following are some of the reasons why we should not exploit animals for people's benefit.

To begin with, some animal-based scientific experiments are entirely cruel and barbaric. Students, for instance, use animals in school to conduct experiments during biology class. Sadly, this also teaches students how to mistreat animals. **It has** even **been reported that** some businesses hire hunters to kill animals illegally for the purpose of conducting experiments. Killing an animal contributes to the further degradation of the ecosystem. Unfortunately, humans are destroying the environment by deliberately killing animals without considering the long-term implications of their actions.

Secondly, many experiments on animals are carried out to test cosmetic products which we do not need. Using innocent animals to test cosmetics that we do not need is not only unethical and cruel, but it is also irresponsible. As a society, we need to learn how to respect and preserve nature.

While it is true that using animals is helpful when conducting medical research, some volunteers are willing to participate in experiments in exchange for payment. This means that there is no need to conduct experiments on animals since better alternatives are available.

As mentioned above, using animals to benefit humankind is unacceptably cruel, and viable alternatives are available. It is horrifying that, as a society, we do not regard the killing of innocent animals in experiments as unacceptable. Yet, we would cringe at the thought of doing the same with humans. We must learn to respect animal lives in the same way that we respect human lives.

Essay Template 18

Traditional games are better than modern games when it comes to assisting children in the development of their skills.

Do you agree with this statement?

Generally, it is commonly believed that traditional games are superior to modern games in aiding the development of a child's skills and abilities. The following are some of the reasons why I find this to be untrue.

In today's world, children need to develop skills that will help them control electronic devices, navigate software, and solve problems, among other things. Learning these skills is a primary requirement for success. Modern games involve the use of electronic devices. Utilizing such devices can help you keep up with the modern technologies widely used in everyday life.

It is also important to note that modern games cultivate team spirit and the ability to collaborate with other people. Being able to collaborate with other people is a crucial skill in any organization. Many jobs require workers to **operate** as virtual team members, just like in modern video games. If they have developed this skill by the time they leave school, they will stand a greater chance of finding employment. **Furthermore,** since video games have increased in popularity, being familiar with these technologies can even result in careers in video game design or animation. Playing modern games may even increase the number of job opportunities available to young people in the future.

I strongly believe that modern games can assist young people in developing important skills. Therefore, modern games should be given precedence over traditional games. While there are some traditional games, like chess, that can aid in developing independent thinking skills in children; the ability to think independently may be developed in a variety of other ways, such as through reading.

Essay Template 19

The number of people moving from rural to urban areas in search of a better life is increasing, but city life comes with its own set of issues.

What exactly are these issues, and how can they be solved?

**The following two essays are exactly the same, except for the organization. Choose the one you are most comfortable with.

<u>Sample Structure 1</u>

A growing number of people are relocating from rural to urban areas in search of a better quality of life. However, problems such as housing shortages, traffic congestion, and pollution can seriously impact that quality of life. This essay will examine these issues and propose potential solutions.

Firstly, the dense concentration of people in cities has resulted in a shortage of affordable housing. In several large cities, for example, many people end up living in the suburbs since the shortage of space means renting in the city is too expensive. Living far away from work forces people to commute daily, which contributes to the second issue, traffic congestion. Traffic congestion has become a critical issue in several cities worldwide. In Shanghai, for example, if you want to go from the East to the West, you may end up spending seven hours sitting in your car due to traffic jams. Overpopulation and excessive traffic lead to pollution, which is the third issue to be addressed. As a result of the high population density in cities, air and water pollution problems are more prominent than in rural areas. This can lead to numerous health risks and can reduce quality of life.

As a first step, governments should provide more affordable housing in city centers. For example, UK cities like Manchester and London have government housing near the city centers to assist low-income families. Another thing that the government must improve is transportation infrastructure to manage traffic volume. Many people commute daily, so having efficient public transport is crucial to enhance the quality of life. **Finally**, local governments could encourage residents to be more mindful of the environment through events and information campaigns, for instance. Another possible solution is the implementation of car-free zones. **This initiative** has already been launched in several major cities worldwide, and it has had a significant impact on air quality.

In summary, population growth in cities around the world is causing several issues. To address them, we should do everything we can to offer affordable housing in urban areas, improve transportation, and make people aware of our lifestyle's impact on the environment.

Essay Template 20

Life expectancy has been growing in several countries over the past few decades.

What kind of issues will this cause for society? Provide some solutions.

In several countries, the average life expectancy has increased significantly in recent years. This essay will focus on the problems that this trend has caused and come up with some practical solutions. Multiple problems arise as a result of an increase in average life expectancy.

First of all, an aging population puts a significant strain on the government. Taxpayers will have to support an aging population that can no longer work financially. To prevent this, increased emphasis should be placed on a more sensible distribution of government funds. The government should invest less money in space exploration and other non-essential projects. Instead, they should use this money to assist the aging population.

Furthermore, as fewer people have children, fewer young people will care for the elderly in the future. The government should provide people with financial incentives to have more children to achieve a more balanced population. Various countries have successfully implemented similar strategies in the past.

Finally, living longer may result in lower quality of life in many cases due to ongoing health issues. Therefore, the well-being of the elderly should be prioritized. It is essential to provide them with ways to participate in activities, such as learning a new skill or a hobby. Our entire society should work together to help senior citizens improve their quality of life.

In summary, the rise in average life expectancy has caused a slew of issues. Therefore, we should start taking appropriate measures, such as better allocating government funds, encouraging people to have more children, and providing senior citizens with activities that will make their lives more enjoyable.

Private IELTS Writing Course for BANDS 7-9

https://www.udemy.com/course/ielts-writing-proficiency-9-academic-writing/

FREE IELTS Writing Course: Advanced Writing (Foundation Level for IELTS)

Access the FREE Course Below!

https://www.macsonbell.com/ielts-toolbox

About the Author

MARC ROCHE is a Legal English Trainer and examiner, a Business Writing Coach, and an IELTS exam prep specialist, as well as a writer and entrepreneur.

He has worked with organizations such as the British Council, the Royal Melbourne Institute of Technology and University of Technology Sydney, among others. Marc has also collaborated with multinationals such as Nike, GlaxoSmithKline and Bolsas y Mercados.

Marc is originally from Manchester, England..

Marc studied Business Management & Business Law at university, before gaining his teaching qualification.

In his free time, he likes to travel, cook, write, play sports, watch football (Manchester City and Real Madrid) and spend time with friends and family.

Learn more about Marc at
amazon.com/author/marcroche

FREE training resources for students and teachers
https://www.macsonbell.com/free-toolbox-sign-up-form

Made in the USA
Middletown, DE
25 July 2024

57998853R00198